Shannon

Rita & Ed ~
you will find
this disturbing in places,
but read on & let me
know what you
think.

Mary xoxox
& Bruno

Shannon

The incredible true story of one girl's
journey from darkness to light

As told by
Damaris Kofmehl

Hodder & Stoughton
LONDON SYDNEY AUCKLAND

Unless otherwise indicated, Scripture quotations are taken from the
HOLY BIBLE, NEW INTERNATIONAL VERSION.
Copyright © 1973, 1978, 1984 by International Bible Society.
Used by permission of Hodder & Stoughton. All rights reserved.
'NIV' is a registered trademark of International Bible Society.
UK trademark number 1448790.

Shannon – ein wildes Leben first published in the German language
by Brunnen Verlag Basel, Switzerland.

Copyright © 2000 by Brunnen Verlag Basel
English language translation copyright © 2002 by Rebecca Beard

First published in Great Britain in 2002

The right of Damaris Kofmehl to be identified as
the Author of the Work has been asserted by her in accordance
with the Copyright, Designs and Patents Act 1988.

10 9 8 7 6 5 4 3 2

British Library Cataloguing in Publication Data
A record for this book is available from the British Library

ISBN 0 340 78648 5

Typeset by Avon Dataset Ltd, Bidford-on-Avon, Warks

Printed and bound in Great Britain by
Bookmarque Ltd, Croydon, Surrey

Hodder & Stoughton
A Division of Hodder Headline Ltd
338 Euston Road
London NW1 3BH

Contents

A note to the reader

Shannon's story is a true story, although the names of some individuals and places have been changed. The only other qualification to this is the fact that certain passages have had to be glossed over and toned down. This is because readers would have found an accurate, true-to-life description of Shannon's experiences difficult to stomach and almost impossible to deal with. An overly realistic portrayal of the full extent of Shannon's experiences throughout her young life is unthinkable. Even in its present form it is hard enough to take.

Furthermore, readers will continually be surprised by just how *young* the children and young people are in this book, and yet how 'grown-up' they seem in the way they speak, think and behave on many occasions. Indeed, this simply doesn't seem to compare with the development of a 'normal' European youngster. But there is a reason for this: the children and young people described here all found themselves out on the street from a very, very young age. In order to manage to survive at all, they had to learn to lead wholly independent and self-reliant lives. These children were left to themselves: they had neither human protection nor a home. They had no parents or family to give them support and security. And thus, for example, many of these ten- and thirteen-year-old girls have had a far wider (and more traumatic) exposure to the world than would be normal for a girl in our western society at the age of twenty. If you look at photos of these kinds of young people, you often have the feeling that you are looking into the faces of grown-ups . . .

Damaris Kofmehl

1

Dad

'Sit still, Shannon!'

'Yes, Aunt Carolina.'

'And take that chewing-gum out of your mouth!'

'Yes, Aunt.'

The nine-year-old girl stuck the chewing-gum provocatively on to the seat in front of her, earning herself a hefty box around the ears.

'That's enough! Do you think I've got nothing better to do than to fly to the United States with a cheeky little brat like you?'

Shannon held her burning cheek and looked sulkily ahead.

'And just so that you know: your father's not the great hero you take him for. He'll soon cure you of your bad manners, I can guarantee you that!' She nodded to the chewing-gum. 'Get rid of that – please!'

The girl pretended not to hear the demand.

'Shall I get the steward?' Aunt Carolina was threatening her wilful niece in an effort to demonstrate her authority – to the other passengers, at least.

An older, rather plump man sitting diagonally across from her laid down his newspaper, looked haughtily over his glasses at the young woman, and said with all the authority of a long life: 'Young people are no longer what they were. In our day we still respected grown-ups. And if we didn't do what we were told, we were given a good hiding. No half-measures, that's what I say.'

'Thank you,' replied the aunt drily, 'I am not responsible for this girl's bad upbringing. If I'd had my way the child would have stayed with her grandparents in Brazil, anyway. What's she going to do in the USA with her father, a man she's never set eyes upon before?' She shook her head. 'No good will come of it. But nobody ever listens to me.'

Shannon stared sullenly at the chewing-gum on the seat in front of her, an outward sign of the tension within, and tried to ignore her aunt's bitter remarks. Aunt Carolina hadn't a clue anyway, she thought. Her father was the best man alive, that much was clear. Up until recently her aunt had even said as much herself – indeed, not only Aunt Carolina, but the whole family as well: Aunt Fernanda, Aunt Sara, Uncle Felipe and, of course, Grandma and Grandad.

'Your father is a fine person,' her grandmother said vaguely every time Shannon asked about him. And that happened a lot. Because Shannon wanted precise information. After all, there had to be some reason why she couldn't live with her parents, like other children.

'If my father is a fine person, why don't I live with him?'

'That's not possible, Shannon,' replied her grandmother. 'How many times have I already told you: your father is a very busy man. You would only be in his way. And you don't want that, do you?'

'And what about my mother?' Shannon would dig deeper. 'Why can't I live with her?'

'That's not possible either.'

'But why not? You said yourself she lives very close to my father.'

'You shouldn't keep asking questions, child,' the grandmother would say in an attempt to put an end to her granddaughter's curiosity. 'Don't you like it with us?'

'Yes, I do.'

'Then do me a favour, and stop worrying about your parents. They have their reasons for leaving you with us. But you're too young to understand.' And yet again that would be her grandmother's final word on the unpleasant topic. Shannon knew her grandmother well enough to know that it would not be a good idea to question her further. When Grandma drew the line it was better just to accept this without questioning and postpone the conversation until another time. Shannon was already well practised in this because questions about her parents whirled endlessly around in her head, and if Grandma hadn't made her pointed dislike of these interrogations so obvious, then Shannon would probably have pumped her unremittingly. There was so much that Shannon wanted to know. So much that was hard to understand. And the grown-ups always bought her off with promises of explaining it all when she was older.

'You're too young for that,' was the most common answer to her burning questions. Shannon hated this answer. It wasn't fair that adults could fend off children with this sentence when a topic came up that was too tricky for them. These were her parents she was always asking about, and with that, of course, her own history. And yet nobody seemed to know anything about it, or to even want to know anything about it. There were things that were simply not discussed. And it was as if her own memory of her life before she came to live with her grandparents had been simply erased. That was not so very surprising: when her father had bundled her off to Brazil she hadn't even been two years old – one year and ten months exactly. At least that's what she was told later on. Amazingly enough, she even had a broken memory of the farewell scene, as if she were remembering a film where some of the sequences had been cut, or a dream where the people were all faceless . . .

She is clinging on to a teddy bear as she enters the huge airport building on her tiny, wobbly little legs, holding her father's hand. Suddenly the father snatches the bear and throws it far away. Instinctively the girl runs after her precious teddy, picks it up from the floor, hugs it to her in her little arms, and then goes to return to her father. But when she looks around for him, he is no longer there. He has simply disappeared, without saying goodbye, without giving his daughter one final parting kiss on the cheek, without in any way preparing her for the separation. And before she has properly realised what is going on, a strange woman is gripping her tightly, dragging her off and taking her to Brazil.

That was all that Shannon could remember.

The following year, her father brought his girlfriend of the time, Alice, to visit her in Ribeirão Preto, the town where Shannon was living with her grandparents. But Shannon could hardly remember the visit. The link to her father only began to become important to her when he started ringing her up. Admittedly, this didn't happen terribly frequently – only at Christmas and on her birthday, in fact. But for Shannon those telephone conversations with her father were the greatest. They gave her the indescribable feeling of being in some way important to him. Once, he even sent her money for a bicycle! It was her first bicycle, and she would always be proud of it.

Her father had given it to her! *Her* father! And often there were times when she wished for nothing more dearly than for her father to come and take her back with him to the United States – even though she knew it wasn't possible.

And then a couple of weeks ago he had rung up again. It was on 17th December 1980, Shannon's ninth birthday. This day was to change Shannon's life, although not in the way Shannon had imagined . . .

'Hello, my princess!' came his voice from a distance of 8,000 kilometres over the phone line. 'Happy birthday!'

'Hello, Dad!' replied Shannon happily, and her father's rough but familiar voice made her heart beat momentarily faster. 'I was sitting by the telephone the whole time, waiting for you to call.'

'How are you, then?' asked her father. 'Are you working hard at school?'

'More or less.'

'And how's your grandmother?'

'Fine.' Shannon wasn't surprised that he only asked about Grandma. He never lost too many words on his father, her grandfather, who was the bane of the whole family. There wasn't a single relative he hadn't managed to stir into a rage with his provocative remarks. Grandma, who had an explosive temperament anyway, had even gone for him with a knife once when he called her a whore. He had accused her of cheating on him when *he* was the one who was seeing another woman behind her back and giving nearly all the company's money to his mistress.

'I miss you, Dad,' whispered the nine-year-old into the receiver. 'Why don't you come and visit me?'

'I'm afraid that's not on,' replied her father, but in a promising tone he added, 'although I may just have a much better idea.'

'What kind of an idea?'

'Of course, I can't force you. It's entirely up to you. I'd be absolutely delighted, that's for sure. But perhaps you'll think it's a very bad idea.'

Shannon began to move around impatiently on the chair.

'What kind of an idea?'

'I just thought . . . of course I've thought long and hard about this . . . and I don't know if your grandmother will agree with it . . . and, like I said, perhaps you won't like it at all . . .'

'What, Dad?'

'That you might like to come and live with me, Shannon.'

For a moment the line was absolutely silent. Shannon could feel her heart pulsing right into the very tips of her fingers; the telephone receiver was burning at her ear. What had her father just said?

'Do you really mean it?'

'I'd never joke about such a thing.'

'You want me to come and live with you?'

'Yes.'

'For ever?'

Her father hesitated for a moment. 'Provided you agree.'

Shannon laughed. 'What a question, Dad! I always wanted to come and live with you! Ever since I can remember! When can I come?'

'Calm down, Shannon. Put your grandmother on to me first, so that I can tell her about my plans.'

'Grandma!' Shannon put the receiver down on the table at once and rushed out of the room. 'Grandma! My dad wants to speak to you! I'm going to go and live with him!' Her staggering news resounded throughout the whole house. Shannon flitted from one room to another like a dancing butterfly. She wanted to tell everyone about it, straight away. News like this just couldn't wait.

Uncle Felipe was sitting, in his wheelchair in his room, as gloomy as ever; he seemed to be brooding over the unfair distribution of human misfortune. When Shannon flung open the door, he started up in his usual cross manner:

'You should knock before you enter. How many times do I have to tell you?'

'I'm going to go and live with my dad!' Shannon announced, ignoring her uncle's ill-temper. 'Have you seen Grandma anywhere?'

'What do I care about your grandmother?' muttered her uncle irritably. 'Look for her yourself and leave me in peace.'

Shannon rushed out of the room.

'And kindly close the door, there's a draught!'

But out of sheer excitement Shannon forgot such a minor point, and her uncle cursed her as she carried on looking for her grandmother.

In the television room she found Aunt Fernanda, who also lived in the Ribeiro family's generously sized house. She was into alternative living, and spent most of her time doing yoga. She sat with her legs crossed on the floor, her hands on her knees in receiving position, her eyes closed and apparently in a trance. Naturally, she was everything but enthusiastic when Shannon awoke her rather rudely from her deep meditation.

'Do you know where Grandma is?'

'Have you been totally abandoned by all the good spirits? What are you thinking of, breaking up my transcendental aura so abruptly?'

'I'm sorry, Aunt. But it's important: I'm going to go and live with my dad!'

'For heaven's sake,' gasped Aunt Fernanda, and all signs of transfiguration vanished from her face. 'Who's been telling you such rubbish?'

'It's not rubbish. My dad wants me to go and live with him in the USA!'

'For heaven's sake,' said her aunt for the second time, 'does your grandmother know about this yet?'

'No. But that's why I'm looking for her. My dad's on the phone and wants to talk to her about it.'

'It had to happen,' Aunt Fernanda muttered to herself. Then she got up quickly and pushed the girl to the door. 'Your grandmother will be delighted.'

They met Grandma together with Aunt Carolina in the back yard. Both women had their backs to them and were standing at the stone water trough, rubbing a few clothes with a lot of soap and dedication. Samanta, a German shepherd dog, was lying panting under a coconut tree in the middle of the big yard, surveying her royal estate peaceably. The tarmacked ground was littered with the empty beer bottles and cigarette butts they had forgotten to clear up from the last party. There were parties at the Ribeiros' nearly every evening. Relatives and acquaintances from both near and far met up here spontaneously for an evening of cheerful music and chat. They always drank until late into the night, dancing the samba and partying, and Shannon was always right in the middle of it all. Loud music, cheerful laughter, so many people in a good mood – that was just her sort of thing!

'Grandma!' Shannon called out before she had even reached the yard. 'My dad wants me to go to the USA!' The rhythmic noise of the clothes brushes stopped immediately, and the two women turned around.

'What did you just say?' asked her grandmother, a tall, slim woman who, despite her age, had lost none of the sharp pride that had been bestowed on her almost as a birthright by her Italian family. Her facial features spoke of a life marked by hardship and frustration. But her eyes flamed with the stubborn will of a wild horse.

'Francisco has gone crazy,' was Aunt Fernanda's comment. 'First of all he leaves Shannon here, and now he wants her back again.'

'Who says so?' asked Aunt Carolina.

'Our favourite brother,' said Fernanda. 'Shannon's father. He's on the phone.'

Shannon's grandmother didn't say a word. But her concern was obvious from her face. She wiped her wet hands on her skirt as, with an indefinable look, she took in Shannon from head to toe. Then she let the washing be, and strode determinedly into the house. Shannon stood rather awkwardly, feeling the critical gazes of her aunts weighing down on her.

'What are you staring at me for? He's my dad, after all!'

'You don't know your father,' Aunt Fernanda said drily.

'I do so!' countered the nine-year-old. 'You're the ones who don't know him.'

'I've known your father since he was in nappies,' returned Fernanda, 'and I tell you: you don't know what you're letting yourself in for.'

'You just want to mess it all up for me,' growled Shannon and folded her arms, hurt. 'I'm going to go and live with my dad. And that's that.'

Now it was Aunt Carolina's turn. She was twenty-seven years old and an energetic biology student. She knelt down next to Shannon and took her by the arm.

'Listen here, Shannon. We don't want to ruin anything for you. We just want what's best for you.'

'Then let me go and live with my father.'

'But that's just what's *not* best for you.'

Shannon wriggled free from her aunt's grip and took a step

back. 'And how do you know what's best for me? It's *my* life! And he's *my* father!'

'Shannon,' Carolina tried another approach, 'you last saw your father when you were *three* years old. And you hear his voice a whole *two* times a year. That's all. You've never been worth more than that to your father.'

'He had a lot to do.'

'Exactly! And that's not going to change when you go and live with him in the USA. Your father doesn't have any time for you, don't you understand that?'

No, Shannon didn't understand that. And it made her mad that her aunts spoke about her father as if he were incapable of making the right decision himself.

'My father knows what he's doing. And you're all just stupid!'

'Your father is a businessman! He's not going to put his career on the line for you!'

'He's the best, the very best! You're just jealous of him!' With these words Shannon ran past her aunts into the house. She was mad. It was her perfect right to go and live with her father, and she was going to do just that, regardless of what her relatives thought. She headed straight for the guestroom where her grandmother was speaking to her father on the telephone. When Shannon entered the room, the old woman ended the conversation pretty abruptly and hung up. Once again, she sized up the nine-year-old girl with peculiar seriousness. Shannon was nearly bursting with curiosity.

'And? What did he say? When am I flying out?'

Her grandmother pushed a strand of grey hair back from her forehead.

'So you think your father's going to meet you with open arms?' she ascertained drily.

'He's a great person. That's what you always said, isn't it, Grandma?'

'Sure,' murmured Grandma, but for the first time it didn't sound terribly convincing. 'And what about school? And your friends?'

'But I can go to school there. And I'm sure I'll make friends as well.' Shannon would miss her family and life in Brazil, but there was no way she was going to miss the opportunity to live with her dad. She went up to her grandmother, hugged her and looked pleadingly up at her with her big dark eyes. 'Please, Grandma. Say you'll let me go, please!'

Her grandmother was silent for a while, then gave a deep sigh and stroked her granddaughter's dark curly hair.

'I'm afraid I don't have any other choice,' she said eventually. 'He's your father. The law's on his side now.'

Shannon gave an enthusiastic whoop and gave her grandmother an almighty kiss on the cheek.

Like a whirlwind she raced from the house to tell everyone the staggering news. Most of all, she had to tell Adriano. Adriano was her cousin and lived with his parents and three brothers and sisters just over the street. He was her best friend. Together they had hatched the craziest of tricks, and when she and Adriano sped through the place on his motorbike she felt invincible. He was several years older than her and suffered from schizophrenia, which meant that most people didn't want to have anything to do with him. Once they had gone swimming together, and he had nearly drowned Shannon in one of his uncontrollable fits; she had been fished out of the river blue in the face. Nevertheless, Shannon loved her cousin as if he were her brother, and not even his mental illness could weaken the bond of their friendship.

Unlike Adriano, his three siblings didn't have a good word to say about Shannon. They found it completely unacceptable that she was spoiled and pampered by the whole extended family, just because she came from the USA and didn't know her parents. Michel and Carlos sometimes told her they would train Samanta, the sheepdog, to eat her up, and Shannon was terrified that they really would do it. But most of all she was afraid of Larissa. Larissa was a year and a half older than Shannon and seemed to spend all her free time thinking of how to get her own back on her cousin. She hated Shannon to the core. Her jealousy was almost neurotic, especially when Shannon got the same presents as she did or was allowed to go on holiday with her family. Once she threw a wooden ladder on top of Shannon, and ran away giggling when the younger girl began to cry. Another time she poured a bucket of water over her cousin's head when Shannon was washing her clothes. But on that occasion Grandma grabbed Larissa by the collar and ordered Shannon to punish the girl by throwing a bucket of water over her head in return. When Shannon hesitated, not wanting to do this, her grandmother threatened to empty a second bucket of water over her head if she didn't avenge herself immediately. And because Shannon knew her grandmother's temper only too well, she ultimately obeyed her, knowing full well that this would only stir Larissa's jealousy still further.

But on this evening, when Shannon, beside herself with happiness, stormed breathlessly into their house and told the whole family that she was going to go and live with her father in the USA, the brothers and sisters didn't make any unkind remarks for once, and even wished her luck. They were only too happy that she was finally clearing off. Adriano was the only one who said nothing. If Shannon left them, then that meant he would slip back into the role of the outsider, the role of the mentally ill, unstable one. In Shannon he would undoubtedly be losing a little sister, and that hurt, even though he didn't show it, instead remaining conspicuously silent.

On the other hand Aunt Sara, the mother of the four children, showed the same concern in her face as Aunt Fernanda, Aunt Carolina and Grandma. She obviously wasn't very happy about the situation either; she too seemed to suspect that the invitation to the USA was going to cause problems, terrible problems. But Shannon didn't want to hear anything of that sort. Her father had given her the best birthday present ever, of this she was convinced. And no one could tell her otherwise.

Not until she had said goodbye and already left the house did Adriano come running after her and grab hold of her arm.

'When will you come back again?' he asked hesitantly. Shannon shrugged her shoulders.

'I'll come and visit you, I promise.'

'You won't,' said Adriano, 'you'll forget about me, I know you will.'

'I won't forget you, Adriano. We're friends.'

'You'll forget me all the same,' said her cousin, persisting in his conviction. 'But I don't hold it against you, Shannon. Someone like me is easily forgotten.'

'That's not true,' said Shannon. They stood opposite one another for a while, and suddenly Shannon realised just how much Adriano actually meant to her. But now wasn't the time to get sentimental. On top of that, they would still see one another for a few days before she left.

'I'm going to miss you,' said Adriano, pulling his nine-year-old cousin close to him.

'Me too,' said Shannon quietly.

'For the last time, get rid of that chewing-gum!' Her aunt's demand brought Shannon back to reality. Grudgingly, she stretched out her hand and picked the chewing-gum off the seat in front, extra slowly.

'Is her father Brazilian?' The question came from the fat, older man sitting diagonally across from them.

'Yes,' replied Aunt Carolina, 'but he emigrated to the United States when he was nineteen. I was hardly any older than my niece is today at the time.'

That's none of his business, thought Shannon to herself. He'd be better off reading his newspaper than poking his nose into other people's affairs.

'He broke off all contact with his family,' confided Aunt Carolina. 'And then all of a sudden it turned out that he'd brought a child into the world and was going to send it to us in Brazil.'

'I understand,' said the older man, interested.

You don't understand anything at all, thought Shannon, and if you don't ever shut up, I'll stick this chewing-gum on your stupid bald head.

'Yes,' sighed Aunt Carolina, 'and now, after seven years, he demands his daughter back. Just like that. As if she'd just been with us for a short visit during the holidays. You can imagine that we're not too happy about it.'

'Absolutely.'

'And I was sweet-talked into accompanying my niece.'

'Ah.'

'To make the change easier for her, that was the idea.'

'And how long are you staying?'

'Three to four weeks. At most. I can't stay any longer anyway because of my studies. Thank God.'

Shannon wrapped the chewing-gum in a scrap of paper and let it drop silently to the floor. The ease with which her aunt spoke about her hurt her feelings. It really wasn't necessary to make a spectacle of her in front of everybody just because she stuck her chewing-gum on to the seat in front. Admittedly, she had been difficult during the flight. But she had to give vent to her mixed feelings somehow! She didn't even know herself what she thought of the whole thing. On the one hand, she was looking forward to being with her father, but this was accompanied by such a queasy feeling that she had actually quite lost her appetite. Was she afraid? Afraid of a new life in a completely strange world? Or did she fear, somewhere deep down in her little soul, that her father wasn't quite the man she held him to be?

Whatever it was, it left her almost breathless. She felt so lousy that she spent the whole time thinking she would throw up. Her aunt's comments seemed to make the whole thing even worse.

After several hours the plane finally began its descent into Minneapolis in the US state of Minnesota, and as Shannon looked out of the window at this huge city laid out below her, she was almost dizzy with the thought of what lay ahead.

Her heart was beating like mad as she walked through the automatic glass door and searched the crowd of people looking for a man who was supposed to be her father. Would she recognise him? Impossible. She was only three the last time she saw him. And would he maybe recognise *her*? How would he greet her? Would he whirl her around, the way she had seen in films? He would definitely hug her tightly to him and tell her how tall she'd got. Yes, he would definitely do that.

'There he is, at the back!' said Aunt Carolina suddenly, grabbing Shannon's hand and pushing her way through the crowd. She headed for a couple. The woman had a pushchair with her. That must be Dad's new wife.

And he was standing next to her.

Her father.

He was tall and strong, with short black hair and tanned skin. He was wearing a dark blue winter coat, worn-out jeans and trainers. His hands were thrust into his trouser pockets, and as Shannon made her way hesitantly towards him, his big black eyes sized her up from head to toe. Shannon felt his gaze resting on her, and felt miserable. Of course he thought she was ugly. Of course he hadn't imagined his daughter to be so small and pale and thin. And then this awful blue sailor dress and this terrible big ribbon in her messy hair! Shannon felt incredibly stupid. She would much rather have worn her favourite green jumper and old jeans. But Grandma thought she should look extra special when she met her father, and had bought her this terrible dress and thrown out all her old clothes without even asking.

'*Oi, irmão,*' said Aunt Carolina, greeting her brother in Portuguese. There was a distinct lack of emotion.

'Hi, sister,' replied Francisco equally drily in English, shaking his sister's hand casually, as if he were shaking the hand of a business partner who had just returned from vacation. It was as if the two had seen each other only yesterday – yet it was six years since they had last met! Now her father turned to Shannon, and as their eyes met she could feel her face turning red.

'And so you are my Shannon,' he said, catching her hand. 'Welcome to the United States of America!' Shannon looked at him in amazement, and a smile flashed across his face. 'That's English, my little one. That will be your language from now on.' He pointed to the woman with the pushchair. 'And that's Valerie, your stepmother.'

'Hi, little girl,' Valerie said sweetly, reaching out her hand. Shannon took her hand distrustfully, and murmured a soft 'hello'.

'And this here is Melissa, your half-sister,' her father introduced the youngest member of the family, who was sleeping peacefully in the pushchair. 'And we're planning for another baby next year, isn't that right, Valerie?' He hugged his wife from behind, put his hands on her stomach and kissed her gently. Shannon looked at her stepmother aggressively. She didn't at all like the way her father hugged this woman so passionately, not when he'd greeted her so coolly. He hadn't even given her a kiss, and he certainly hadn't whirled her around. She had expected it all to be a little warmer. And she didn't much like the prospect of having to learn English, either. She took a step back, clung nervously on to Aunt Carolina and desperately hoped that she wasn't still cross with her over the chewing-gum.

All of a sudden she wasn't at all sure it had been a good idea to come and live with her father. But now there was no way back.

2

The boy with the guitar

From the moment she first laid eyes upon him, she felt herself strangely drawn to him. Yes, there was something mysterious, mystical about him. Something she couldn't describe. He was like something from outer space landed in the middle of this exotic gathering in which her father had left her.

'Run along and play now, my little treasure,' her father had told her, 'I won't be longer than an hour.' And then he had left and not returned. Even though he had promised her he would take time off and travel to the seaside with her. To the beach at Los Angeles. Just him and her. And they had actually taken the plane to Los Angeles and set up home in her uncle's villa, ten kilometres from the sea. But that was three days ago now, and her father still hadn't found any time to make good his promise. Instead, he had always had something important to do in town, and on the first two days he hadn't been back before midnight. And now, on this third evening, just when Uncle Federico was organising a party, he made a spur-of-the-moment decision to go out with friends and leave her once more to her own devices.

Usually Shannon loved being at parties. In her grandparents' back yard she hadn't missed a single one, and had joked around with the grown-ups until late into the night. But this time it was different – irritating. Here there was also drink and laughter, but the guests, in every word they said, in every movement they made, indeed in their whole appearance in general, seemed somehow disturbing, just like the host himself. Perhaps it had something to do with the fact that Uncle Federico was a 'Satanist', as Shannon's father had told her. The nine-year-old didn't understand what was meant by that, but she knew that she felt an eerie chill every time he as much as came near her. He was a tall, heavily built man, and always wore eccentric clothes, either in flame-red or coal-black combinations. He never laughed, and his face always carried the same chilling, calculating expression. And yet the guests all gathered around him as if he possessed powers that made him some kind of higher being. Shannon found a little place for herself in a corner where she would not be noticed, and waited for the party to end.

And then she saw the boy with the guitar. It was hard to guess his age. Perhaps fourteen. Or sixteen. In any case, considerably younger than all the other guests, and considerably less well turned out: thin, with long brown uncombed hair. He seemed to have wandered mistakenly into this gathering, like a soap-bubble in a high security prison. Shannon certainly couldn't understand what a boy like him was doing here. He was sitting, just like her, on a bench to one side of the main turmoil, cigarette stuck in the corner of his mouth, strumming distractedly on his guitar and gazing rather vacantly at the roof. He was wearing a white South American cotton shirt, elasticated violet trousers and sandals. A gold chain dangled from his neck.

Shannon watched him for a while. He looked straight at her once, but she wasn't sure whether he had really seen her or just stared right through her. In any case, he stood up suddenly, took his guitar and disappeared. Shannon pulled at one of the curls from her brown shock of hair, and wound it round and round her index finger as she distractedly surveyed the mass of guests without any great interest. They were all concerned only with themselves. She would have bet good money that not one of them had noticed a nine-year-old girl sitting lonely and silently in the corner. And if the girl had suddenly fallen lifeless to the floor, they wouldn't have noticed that, either.

'Hi, do you want a drink?'

Shannon gave a start. None other than the boy with the guitar was standing in front of her, offering her a can of Coca-Cola.

'Thanks,' mumbled Shannon, wondering where the boy had found a can of Coke, because she herself had looked unsuccessfully on the drinks table for one earlier.

'Can I join you?' asked the boy. Shannon nodded, and moved over on the black-painted bench. The boy sat with the guitar on his knee and quietly began improvising a song.

'How do you like it here in the United States?' he asked, as if the words were part of the song he was strumming. Shannon was perplexed.

'How do you know . . . ?'

'Your accent betrays you.'

'Oh.'

The boy plucked skilfully at the guitar strings and nodded in time to his music.

'So, do you like it? Or do you want to go back to Brazil?'

'How do you know that I come from Brazil?'

The boy tapped his temple with his index finger. 'Intuition.'

'Aha!' responded Shannon, even though she had no idea what intuition was.

'You're Federico's niece, is that right?'

'How do you know that?' repeated Shannon in wonder. But the boy merely blew a bleached strand of hair out of his face.

'You haven't answered my question.'

'Which question?'

'If you like it here.'

'Oh, right. Yes. I do.'

'You don't sound so terribly convinced.'

'I haven't been here very long.'

'All the same.' The boy twanged discordantly on his guitar and with raised eyebrows peered out at the girl from under his drooping fringe. 'Problems with your father?'

Shannon was confused. These boy's questions were just too precise.

'What do you know about my father?'

'So you are having problems, then?

'No, I'm not,' the girl asserted. 'My father and I get along just great.'

'Oh yes.'

'He's the best father I can imagine.'

The boy stopped playing and suddenly began to laugh. It was a strange laugh. The sympathetic laughter of the initiated at the newcomer's naivety.

'You'll start to wonder,' he said mysteriously. 'You'll really start to wonder.'

He didn't seem to take Shannon's praise of her father at all seriously. And he seemed to have his reasons for this. That made Shannon think.

'Who are you?' she asked him uncertainly. The boy tossed back his long hair and gave Shannon his hand.

'Robby,' he introduced himself. 'Thirteen years old, single and particularly keen on the supernatural.'

'I'm Shannon.'

'I know.'

Shannon was reeling from one surprise after another. 'How do you know my name?'

'The wind whispered it to me,' he said in hushed, knowing tones, and Shannon gradually began to feel that this Robby, with his eccentric sense of humour, was almost giving her the creeps.

'Who are you really?' she asked.

Robby leaned his head to one side and looked thoughtfully at Shannon's profile for a while. He seemed to be really considering a serious answer.

'I'd like to be a friend to you,' he said finally, and for the first time Shannon had the impression he really meant it. 'Someone you can trust with things you'd never tell anyone else.'

'And why should I trust you?'

Robby leant his chin on his guitar, and again took his time answering.

'Because I understand you better than you do yourself,' he replied philosophically, looking deep into Shannon's big black eyes. He nodded, as if he himself were impressed with his speech. And then he got up abruptly, imparted the prediction that they would certainly bump into each other again, and left.

Shannon didn't know what she should make of him. With the best will in the world, she couldn't size him up. He was so different, so impenetrable and yet so fascinating. And even though they had only spoken to each other for a few minutes, she felt as if they had known one another for years.

'Robby,' Shannon murmured his name, as if the name itself were already part of a huge puzzle that was shrouded in mystery. Privately, she was hoping she would see him again soon to find out more about him — about him and that source of detailed information he had on her.

★   ★   ★

Three weeks later she saw him again. Uncle Federico was giving another party, and this time he had even invited gurus and mediums from Africa and India. Shannon was sitting on the same black bench, winding her hair around her index finger and staring vacantly ahead. She didn't hear Robby coming, and gave a slight start when he spoke to her.

'Hi, Shannon,' he said, as if he'd only just left her to pop to the bathroom and back again since he last saw her. Then he sat down next to her as if it was the most natural thing in the world and straight away began to play on his guitar. He looked just as unkempt as he had done three weeks before. The only thing that had changed was his eyes. They were strangely red and shining. 'Your father's deserted you again, eh?'

Once again, he'd hit the nail on the head. But she didn't want to admit that to him.

'He's always got a lot to do,' she said in defence of her father.

'Obviously,' agreed Robby. 'And you'd much rather go home, right?' He probably didn't know that he'd hit upon the really sore spot. But this is exactly what he'd done. Shannon pursed her lips, and said nothing. Yet she could have screamed. Yes, she wanted to go home. She wanted to go back to Brazil! She wanted to go back to her friends, to her family! She wanted to speak Portuguese again! She wanted to climb the palm tree in the back yard again and play Tarzan. She wanted to go to the pizzeria again with Adriano, stuff herself with pizza and then run away at his command, so as not to have to pay the bill. She wanted to speed with him all over the place on his motorbike, or steal mandarins with him from the market. How she longed to return! And how she longed for the Brazilian food, the samba she used to dance every evening in the back yard, the good humour of the Brazilian people and the shared frenzy during an important football match, an occasion which brought entire businesses to a standstill. There was so much that she missed, and on many an evening she was so homesick that she cried into her pillow until she finally fell asleep from sheer exhaustion.

Luckily Aunt Carolina was still there. In spite of her claim that she would stay a maximum of three to four weeks, she prolonged her stay indefinitely. Since she was between semesters this wasn't a problem, as she could complete the work she needed to hand in at the beginning of the new semester just as well in Minneapolis. And so she worked on her seminar papers, made herself useful around the house and looked after Shannon and little Melissa, while Shannon's father went to work and Valerie spent most of her time meeting friends for coffee. Aunt Carolina had been Shannon's only refuge over the past month. A lifebuoy on a stormy sea. And just *how* stormy it could get sometimes! Shannon's father flew into a rage at the smallest of things. It was probably his job as an IT consultant that made him so ill-tempered. He said himself that his job at the moment was very stressful, and that he would look for another position. At any rate, Aunt Carolina was an expert at calming down her brother whenever he'd just exploded into another one of his rages over some little trifle. She also pushed for the nine-year-old girl finally to be sent to school, so that she didn't miss the boat and fall behind. And that was when it suddenly occurred to Shannon's father to take her with him to Los Angeles for a few days, before life started getting serious. Just for a few days, mind.

'How long are you actually planning to stay on here?' Robby asked, pulling her back out of her thoughts.

Shannon shrugged her shoulders. 'Haven't a clue.'

'Have you been down to the beach over the last three weeks?'

'A couple of times.'

'So what have you done with the rest of your time?'

Shannon hesitated in replying. Then she said: 'Nothing.'

'Well, that's a heck of a lot,' said Robby. 'Have you at least been getting on with your uncle?'

This question positively stopped Shannon's breathing. Her whole body grew stiff with tension, and she sat with her hands screwed up into fists, as if she had turned to stone on the black bench. The memory of what had happened between her and her uncle over the past few weeks hurt too much. She disgusted herself. At first she hadn't thought anything of it when her uncle sat down next to her on the bed and stroked her curly hair. But then his hands had wandered further, and she hadn't been able to do anything about it, had lain there as quiet as a mouse as her uncle violently pushed himself inside her, hoping all the time that this nightmare would soon be over. It had been humiliating. And she had felt so incredibly dirty. Almost every night the dreadful 'game' repeated itself. The nine-year-old girl was completely at her uncle's mercy – just as she had been with her grandfather, who had abused her from the age of four. When Shannon thought about all of that, she felt sick; the worst thing was that she felt that she herself was to blame for what had happened to her. She had never told anyone about it: being so little at the time, she had blanked it out of her mind. And now, with her uncle, she swore to herself that she would not tell a soul. It was too shameful. And probably nobody would have believed her anyway, not even her father, who was already preoccupied and would probably have flown off the handle at such an insinuation. So it was better to hold her tongue.

'I can't stand Federico,' commented Robby, as yet again Shannon did not respond to his question. 'I only came today to see if you were here.'

Shannon swallowed. It was strange. Along came this

boy with his guitar, simply turned up out of nowhere, and everything that he said, every topic he brought up, somehow seemed to manage to open up every badly healed wound inside her. It was as if this Robby could see right into the very centre of her heart. That threw her. And at the same time, it also gave her the feeling that she could trust him.

He began to play a melancholy tune and looked dreamily at Shannon. 'She came from Brazil to a foreign country,' he sang, making up the text for his song as he went along, never once taking his eyes from her, 'a little girl with big dreams. And the dreams kept her alive. Don't give up, little girl, don't give up, and don't lose sight of your dreams. Because you're lost without your dreams.'

Shannon felt herself getting hot. She could have told *him*. He was the only person she could have told about what Uncle Federico and also her grandfather had done to her. She could have told him how terribly lonely she felt and how desperately she longed to go home to Brazil. She knew that she could have told him, even when there was no logical reason for this. There was something that linked her to this boy, something special, unique. And yet she couldn't quite find the courage to speak, and so remained silent, just as she had done so many times before in her young life. She had held her tongue once too often to be able to break her silence now.

A week later Shannon travelled back to Minneapolis with her father to the small apartment on the third floor of the high-rise building. But she couldn't stop thinking about the boy with the guitar. Every word that he had said to her was etched in her memory, as was his narrow face with those big melancholy eyes. She would never forget those eyes of his. She would be able to tell them from thousands of other eyes, this she was sure of, even if she had only seen the boy twice. He was something special. Yes, he was. And she hoped that she would see him again sometime, even if this did seem highly unlikely.

But you never knew with a boy like Robby.

3

His true face

'I told you to be back at six.'

'Yes, Dad.'

'It's already five minutes *past* six.'

'Yes, Dad.'

Shannon's father came right up close to her and dealt her a hefty box around the ears, bringing tears to her eyes.

'I'm sorry, Dad. I didn't notice the time.'

'When I say six o'clock, then I mean six o'clock. Is that clear?'

Shannon held her burning cheek, still not quite able to believe that this was really happening to her. It was a nightmare. She had only been back from Los Angeles for a few weeks, and she had hoped that her father would finally start behaving normally. But he didn't. Quite the opposite, in fact: he got more aggressive from day to day. There was no 'my princess' or 'my little treasure' now. Her father seemed only to think of one thing: beating up his nine-year-old daughter, and this on the smallest of pretexts. Just like this April Tuesday evening.

'But I was only playing volleyball,' explained Shannon, immediately earning a second blow.

'I said six o'clock,' reprimanded her father, and before she knew what was going on, he had grabbed her by the hair and was dragging her roughly into the living room.

Shannon began to cry. 'Let go of me!'

Her father took no notice of her. 'I'll soon cure you of your bad manners, that's for sure!' He rammed her violently against the dining table, and Shannon cracked her back on the edge of it. The pain winded her for a couple of seconds, but before she could run away from her father, he had already locked her in his grip again and was shaking her like a doll.

'*I* make the rules around here, get it? I'm not letting a cheeky little brat like you run rings round me! Is that clear!'

'Stop that right now, Francisco!' It was Aunt Carolina's voice. She came racing out of the kitchen in her apron and, barely pausing for thought, fell on top of her brother and tried to pull him off Shannon. 'You have no right to hit her like that!'

'I wasn't aware that this was any of your business!' snorted Francisco, and pushed Shannon away in order to deal with his sister. Shannon fell backwards on to the ground and crept away into a corner, shaking like a little puppy. Tears were streaming down her face as she watched her father raise himself up in front of her aunt, snorting with indignation.

'She's *my* daughter! And I'll bring her up as *I* see fit!'

'I'll contact the social services and take the child away from you!' said Aunt Carolina in anger.

'The law's on my side.'

'I should never have let Shannon come and live with you!'

'It was her decision to come.'

'Only because you played the superhero with her.'

'I'm her father.'

'You're a lousy pig, Francisco!'

'If you don't like it here, you're welcome to leave. I'm sick to death of you anyway, and so is Valerie! You've intruded enough on our privacy. It's about time you went back to Brazil.'

Aunt Carolina's chest swelled with indignation. She gave her brother a withering look, glanced over at her niece, then lifted her index finger and said in a trembling voice: 'I can guarantee you one thing, brother. If you so much as hurt *one* hair on her head even *once*, I'll have the whole police force after you and make sure you're pulled to pieces.'

Shannon's heart was fit to burst. She thought her aunt looked as if she would start shaking at any moment.

'Get out of my sight!' said her father, in a tone that was not to be argued with. 'Your presence is no longer welcome here.'

Aunt Carolina stood for a while, uncertain, and then looked over again at her niece; when their eyes met, Shannon knew immediately that her aunt had thrown in the towel. The young woman turned away silently and disappeared into her room. Shannon didn't dare move for fear of attracting her father's attention. But he didn't take any notice of her; he went into the bathroom, and Shannon darted to her room as quickly as possible, where she threw herself sobbing on to her bed.

That night Shannon tossed and turned restlessly in her bed and couldn't sleep. She felt a lump the size of a plum stone in her throat. Her back hurt from being banged against the edge of the table, but the pain of it was nothing compared to the pain in her heart.

Aunt Carolina couldn't leave! Not now! She needed her so! How would she survive here without her aunt! With a raving mad father and an explosive stepmother? Right from when she first set eyes upon her at the airport, Shannon hadn't liked Valerie, with her flirtatious laugh and haughty air; over the past weeks her dislike of the woman had only grown.

Aunt Carolina found her difficult as well; Valerie was stiff and arrogant towards her. Perhaps she was jealous because she had noticed that Shannon didn't trust her in the slightest, turning instead to Aunt Carolina for every little thing, even if it was just to have her fingernails cut. Shannon really couldn't stand her stepmother. Sometimes she didn't do what Valerie demanded on purpose, as a way of testing her limits, and when Valerie proceeded to lose her temper Shannon would flee to Aunt Carolina for help, hiding behind her back. It was no surprise the two women were frequently at odds with one another.

But far worse were Aunt Carolina's arguments with Shannon's father. Aunt Carolina had protected her niece from his aggressive, violent behaviour on countless occasions – right up until this Tuesday evening, when Shannon came back late from volleyball. And she'd only been five minutes late, a measly five minutes! But her father had reacted as if it were a hanging crime.

Shannon pressed her face into the pillow to smother her tears. A mixture of fear, faintness and a sense of absolute abandonment squeezed her throat shut. How wrong she had been about her father! How he had tricked her into coming to the USA! That was why everyone had been so concerned when she said she was going to go and live with him. That was why they had talked Aunt Carolina into accompanying her. Because they knew her father. Because they knew perfectly well what he was like. And that was why they hadn't stopped Shannon from going. Because they knew what her father was capable of. They didn't have any other choice. The law was on his side. He was her father. Her father, the man she had been so keen to meet. Her father, the man who had called her 'princess' on the telephone. Her father, the man who treated her like a dog and had just told Aunt Carolina only a few hours ago to go to the devil.

The thought of losing her aunt took the ground away from under her feet, leaving her stunned and senseless. She sobbed into her pillow and wished that this was all just a bad dream from which she would soon awake. She thought about Robby and the song that he had made up for her: 'She came from Brazil to a foreign country, a little girl with big dreams. And the dreams kept her alive. Don't give up, little girl, don't give up, and don't lose sight of your dreams. Because you are lost without your dreams.'

Thinking about Robby made her cry all the harder. Just how did he know how she felt, what was going on inside her, how incredibly lonely she was in this foreign world? She mustn't lose sight of her dreams, he had said. She would be lost without her dreams. But it seemed to be impossible to follow his advice. Where the harsh reality of life had already forced its way into every last corner of a tiny, damaged soul, there was no space left for dreams.

Aunt Carolina left on the following Saturday. With her departure, the very last spark of hope that everything would still turn out for the best died in Shannon.

A few months later, her father took up a new job, and they moved to Cleveland, Ohio, a big city in the middle of the United States, between Detroit and New York. They lived in a spacious house in the city centre. Shannon's room, which she shared with little Melissa, was directly above the garage. A cradle stood in the room next door, because Valerie was expecting another baby in a few weeks' time. Shannon's father and stepmother also had a bedroom on the first floor, as well as an office and a bathroom. A large kitchen, the living and dining rooms and another bathroom were all located on the ground floor. One half of the spacious basement was covered with a green carpet and set up as a cosy television and play room, while the other half was used as a utility and storage room. And there was even a roof terrace. It was a beautiful house, and many of the neighbours were doubtless jealous of it. But Shannon would much rather have lived with a functional family in a hovel than exist unloved in this luxurious house. She had long since learnt that being safe and secure does not necessarily have anything to do with outward appearances, and in her case the one had as much relevance to the other as did a bird of paradise to the North Pole.

Shannon felt the full force of her father's hand ever more frequently. Everything served as a pretext for him to hit his daughter. Even if she simply forgot to turn off the light he would grab her by the hair and bang her head against the wall. One day, Shannon slipped in the bathroom. She stuck out her right hand as she fell, and rather clumsily knocked over a white porcelain duck; just as it shattered on the floor, her father appeared in the doorway. Shannon gave a start when she saw him.

'I . . . I didn't do it on purpose,' she apologised, shaking as she gathered up the broken duck pieces. But her father had no time for apologies.

'You obviously like constantly making a fool of me, eh?' He grabbed Shannon angrily by the scruff of the neck. She was prepared for anything – except for what he had in mind.

'Don't think you're getting away with this,' said her father, and he pushed her thin body up against the toilet and shoved her head violently down the toilet bowl. Shannon felt herself seized by a blind panic. The toilet flushed, and as the water washed down around her head she was temporarily deprived of air. She tried to loosen her father's grip around her neck, but he held her as tightly as if she were in a vice and flushed the toilet for a second time. Shannon panicked, flailing around desperately with her arms. Images shot through her head of

Adriano almost drowning her in the swimming pool during one of his fits.

She wriggled like a worm in an attempt to free herself from her father's grip. But it was to no avail. More and more water poured down over her head, and while her father hurled a tirade of abuse at her, she swallowed, spat and gasped for air. It seemed an eternity before he finally released her, parting with the words: 'Let that be a lesson to you.'

Shannon leaned against the wall and carefully fingered her throat. All of her limbs were still trembling with fright. Her head was spinning, and her chest shook with sudden, uncontrolled sobs. She sat for well over an hour in the bathroom, completely unable to move, arms and legs pulled in tight to her body, as if they formed a wall of defence around a castle. Her tears were the rain, falling on to the wall.

And then Eric came into the world. Shannon was delighted when her half-brother was born. It meant that her stepmother and, more importantly, her father were less focused on her. Now Eric was always the centre of their attention, and she was much freer in her movements around the house. But this luck was not to last for long, and soon the drab reality of everyday life returned, along with her father's terrible temper. Shannon increasingly sought cover behind a display of apathy. She just sat there, staring silently into space and twisting her curls around her fingers.

She also often switched off in school, which she had been attending in Cleveland for the last few weeks. She shut herself off entirely from her surroundings, and when someone dared to come too close to her, she went into defence mode, like a beast of prey protecting its territory. This meant that she fell behind at school, which in turn led to her father beating her even more when the teacher complained. One Thursday

Shannon did so badly in a test that the teacher told her to bring it back the next day signed by her father. On the way home, her feet felt as if they were made of lead. This must be how a prisoner on death row feels when he is walking to the chair, she thought.

The closer to home she got, the heavier her legs became, and by the time she pushed down the door handle she was so frightened of her father's reaction that it was almost unbearable, even though she knew he wouldn't be home yet. Her stepmother was busy in the kitchen, and Melissa was sitting in her highchair, happily stuffing chocolate spread into her dirty little mouth. Shannon stole past the two of them, her school things tucked under her arm, and took the quickest route to her room. She threw her schoolbooks into a corner, sat down on the bed with her heart racing, and nervously began biting her fingernails.

Her father returned home from work two hours later. The mere sound of the door set her pulse racing again. She heard him taking off his shoes, greeting Valerie and then making himself comfortable on the sofa to read the newspaper. Shannon fished the test out of one of her copybooks and looked at it with a feeling of rising nausea. It was a maths test, and Shannon had got all twenty problems wrong. Would it be better to wait until after dinner before showing it to her father? Or should she just get the thrashing out of the way now? She decided to delay the affair for as long as possible and try to wait for a favourable moment, if there was such a thing.

She didn't manage to eat a single bite of her dinner, of course, but the adults didn't notice anything untoward, as she never had a big appetite anyway. Then Shannon had to do the washing-up while her stepmother put Melissa to bed and her father slouched in front of the box. Shannon knew that it was now or never. She fetched the test, mustered all her courage, and shoved it under her father's nose.

'You have to sign this,' she muttered, almost soiling herself with fear.

'What is it?'

'A maths test.'

Her father looked at the pages covered in red ink, and the expression on his face began to change. It was obvious a storm was brewing, and Shannon was already cowering away from the first heavy drops.

'You're not even ashamed of this disgraceful performance, are you?'

Shannon said nothing.

'Would you kindly answer me!'

'I . . .' stammered the girl, 'I'll try to do better next time.'

'You certainly will.' Her father put the test down on the sofa and stood up. As he began to unbuckle his belt, Shannon started to shake like a frightened kitten, and didn't dare move from the spot.

'I'll teach you to bring home decent marks!' shouted her father angrily, raising his arm for the first lash. The belt cracked like a whip as it cut through the air, and Shannon howled out, automatically taking a step back.

'You're a loser!' growled her father. 'A pathetic loser!' With his belt he herded her like a dumb animal to the top of the stairs that led down to the basement. He kept on hitting Shannon until she suddenly lost her balance, fell with a scream down the stairs, and lay sobbing in a heap at the bottom.

'You're good for nothing! Just like your mother!' shouted her father after her. 'It would have been better if you'd never been born!'

Shannon picked herself up, but before she could flee from

her father he was standing over her, beating her mercilessly. This time he didn't just hit her with the belt but kicked her into the bargain. Shannon hid her face in her hands, and screamed and cried.

'You're a nothing!' her father bellowed like a wild animal gone mad, and it seemed as if he was about to work himself up into such a temper that even he wouldn't be able to control it. 'You're a nothing! A nothing!! A nothing!!!' Each word was accompanied by the full force of his foot, and his words hurt just as much as the kicks from his feet.

'Stop it, Dad!' Shannon whimpered desperately. But her father didn't seem to be listening. His voice sound mechanical, eerie.

'A nothing! A nothing! And that's what you'll always be! Always!! Always!! Francisco . . .' Suddenly he broke off. Right in the middle of it. Just as if someone had pulled the emergency brake, or torn the plug from its socket. Only his heavy breathing broke the silence. Shannon peeped out cautiously from between her hands. Dad's feet were right in front of her face, and with pounding heart she steeled herself for the next blow. But it didn't come. Instead, she heard something fall to the ground, and through a chink in her fingers she saw Dad's belt lying on the green carpet next to her bent legs. Something had happened, something unusual, and Shannon didn't know what she should make of it. She knew her father. He had never turned away from her so abruptly. Never.

She saw the feet moving away from her. She ventured to widen the crack between her fingers, and saw her father feeling his way back to the wall and standing there, his hands behind his back and his face strangely contorted.

'Forgive me, Shannon,' she suddenly heard him say, and his voice sounded quite foreign to her. 'I didn't mean to do that. Really I didn't . . . What have I done?' Shannon understood less and less of what was happening. She had never seen her father like this. Never.

'I'm sorry, Shannon,' he continued. 'You have to believe me. I don't want to do this. It's just . . . it's just stronger than me . . . it's . . .' It was almost as if he was about to burst into tears at any moment. 'My father . . . your grandfather often did it to me . . . he . . . he hit me a lot . . . an awful lot . . . and I was too small to defend myself.'

Shannon could taste blood on her lips. She was confused.

'I told myself: when I'm big, I'll pay him back for it . . . and when I was nineteen, I hit out at him in an argument. I knocked him flying, and then he threw me out . . . I came here to the USA.' His voice was clipped, and fragile somehow. It had never sounded like that. It was disconcerting.

'You'll have to forgive me,' he said over and over again, 'you'll have to forgive me.' Then he turned away and went slowly upstairs.

Shannon lay in a heap on the floor, a pitiful bundle of human being, inwardly and outwardly broken and totally devoid of strength. Her whole body ached, but that wasn't why she was sobbing. She was sobbing because she had never felt more wretched. She didn't care if her grandfather had beaten up her father. She already knew that the old man was a pig, she had had personal experience of that. But that didn't give her father the right to vent his anger on *her*. After all, she had never asked to be born into this world, and she hadn't sought out this wretched existence for herself, either. She thought of Robby and how he had laughed when she had claimed that she and her father got along just great. You'll really start to wonder, he had said, and laughed. She could still hear him laughing, and it was almost driving her mad. He had known what lay in store for her, he had simply known, just like Grandma and Aunt Carolina. They had all known – and now she lay crying on the basement floor, covered in bruises because she had messed up a maths test, and there was no one who could help her, no one who could save her from this terrible nightmare. She was completely alone, a nine-year-old girl who longed for nothing more than just to be loved by someone – anyone – in the world.

4

Paul

'Hi!'

Shannon gave an imperceptible jump when the boy spoke to her. 'What's your name?'

'Shannon.'

'How old are you?'

'Ten.'

'You're quite new in this school, aren't you?'

'I've been here three months.'

'Why aren't you with the others?'

'What others?'

'Well, your class friends, for example.'

'I don't have any friends here.'

'Why not?'

'They don't like me.'

'And why don't they like you?

'You can ask them if you want.'

'I will.'

Shannon looked at the boy in surprise. He was tall and thin, and wore a ragged t-shirt with holes in, tattered jeans, battered old trainers and a black leather jacket. He was fair-skinned, with hazel eyes and long, slightly tousled hair. His gaze was somehow cold and dull, yet he was the first boy to strike up a conversation with her in the playground. She had seen him a few times before, but had never actually found out what he did here in the playground. He didn't go to the school, but he often turned up during the longer breaks and mingled with the children. Shannon, for her part, always did the exact opposite: she sat on her own on one of the stone benches, twisted her brown curls around her fingers and waited for the break to end. Nobody wanted to play with her anyway, because she didn't play by the rules. She didn't care any more, and crept off into her own lonely world. But it was a pleasant surprise that this unknown boy seemed to take a particular interest in her. He must have been about as old as Robby, or perhaps a little younger – twelve, maybe thirteen years old.

'What are you doing here?'

'Making contacts,' replied the boy vaguely. 'Not that anyone could say the same of you.'

'What's that got to do with you?' said Shannon testily.

The boy raised his hands in a gesture to cool it. 'All right, all right. I was only saying. I've often noticed you sitting here, and thought you might be lonely.'

'That shouldn't bother you,' Shannon said, surprised that the boy had so obviously observed her on several occasions without her noticing.

'It's horrible being lonely, eh?'

'I'm not lonely.'

'No, of course not.'

'I want to be alone.'

'Nobody chooses to sit on the substitute bench day after day.'

'I can sit wherever I want.'

'Of course you can. But you don't enjoy it, do you?'

'What do you want from me?'

'I thought you might like someone to talk to.'

'Is that what you thought?'

'Share our thoughts, that sort of thing.'

'My thoughts wouldn't interest anybody.'

'How can you know when you're always on your own?'

'I suppose you always know best, do you?'

A smile flitted across the boy's narrow face. 'I know a lot of people,' he said importantly, and put his left foot up on the stone bench, 'people who feel just like you.'

'How do you know how I feel? You don't know me. You don't know anything more about me than my name and my age.'

'You feel cheated.'

Shannon looked at the boy, nonplussed. He had hit the nail on the head. She would never have imagined it could be done so matter-of-factly.

'You can't stand the whole set-up here. You're at your wits' end – with the pupils, the teachers, your family. What you'd most like to do is scream out loud, but nobody would notice and it wouldn't make any difference anyway, so instead you just say nothing at all. Well' – he leaned over her, well aware of his victory – 'do I know how you feel, or am I completely mistaken?'

Shannon, not a little in awe of the accuracy of his description, admitted defeat. 'Okay, you win,' she agreed. 'And now tell me what you're *really* doing here.'

The boy blew a strand of hair casually from his face. 'You'll have to keep it quiet,' he said. 'Can you do that?'

'I never speak with anyone anyhow,' replied Shannon.

The boy nodded towards three boys standing some distance

away, leaning against a tree. Two of them were also wearing black leather jackets, and the third was searching through his trouser pocket.

'We sell drugs,' explained the boy, and spat on the ground.

Shannon's jaw nearly hit the floor. '*What* do you do?'

'It's good business, I can tell you.'

'Are you crazy?'

'Why? You can get drugs at every school. Didn't you know that?'

'Of course I know that,' Shannon lied, as she hadn't had the slightest clue that this was the case. 'But . . . why do you do it?'

'You have to do something.'

'You . . . you simply come here and sell drugs?'

'Yup.'

'Haven't you ever been caught?'

'They can't catch us. Before one of those tottering old teachers arrives on the scene, we're long over the wall.'

'Ah, so you climb over the wall!'

'Did you think we stroll in through the main entrance?' She hadn't thought anything at all, was just a bit thrown by the trade of this boy whose name she didn't even know.

'We don't often come directly into the school yard. We're usually over there.' He nodded towards the gym. 'We're less likely to be disturbed there. But sometimes we risk it out in the middle of the crowd. After all, every school kid is a potential customer. And the bigger the customer base, the larger the profit.'

'You talk as if you were selling chewing-gum. Where do you get the stuff?'

'Contacts,' the boy said simply.

'And . . . what kind of drugs do you sell?'

'Hash, cocaine, heroin, LSD, whatever you fancy, the whole range.'

Shannon was impressed. 'Where do you hide it all? In your leather jacket?'

'Of course, I don't have the whole selection with me. But I have it to order.'

Shannon had never known anyone who sold drugs, and even though she knew the trade was illegal it fascinated her all the same. The boy fascinated her even more. There was something so unbelievably wild about him. And he hadn't been frightened off by her dismissive air, not like all the others. He had seen through her, listened to what she said. That had never happened to her before.

The boy reached into the inner pocket of his jacket and pulled out a hand-rolled cigarette.

'Have you ever smoked one?'

Shannon looked critically at the crumpled cigarette. 'What sort of stuff is that?'

'Hash,' explained the boy. 'Want one?'

Shannon shook her head. 'No, thanks.'

He put the cigarette right under her nose. 'Come on! It's a great feeling. You feel like you're floating, leaving all your problems behind. All of a sudden everything is just cool. And you're not the little, unnoticed Shannon on the substitute bench any more. You can do anything you want, you're the best, the strongest, you're invincible.'

'No, thanks.'

'Hey, what's the problem? Don't you trust me?'

'I don't want to smoke.'

'D'you know how old I was when I smoked my first cigarette? Seven.'

'And?'

'I'll show you what you do.' He lit up the cigarette. 'You breathe in the smoke as deeply as you possibly can. You get the most out of it then.' He took a deep drag, hollowing his cheeks inwards and then blowing the smoke out of his mouth and nose. A strangely sweet odour filled the air.

'Wow,' said the boy, and shut his eyes momentarily with pleasure. 'You don't know what you're missing.'

The bell rang, signalling the end of the break, and the children ran noisily into the school building.

'Ah well, doesn't have to be today,' said the boy, shrugging his shoulders and giving Shannon a friendly wink. 'Time for me to disappear with my buddies.' He looked around for the two boys in leather jackets and nodded to them to come over. They must have been about fifteen or sixteen, although it was difficult to tell; their pale complexions aged them.

'This is Terry and Bob,' the boy introduced his mates. 'Guys, this is Shannon.' They wore faded jeans, and their hair didn't look as if it had been combed for a long time. Terry was tall and scrawny and had small, beady eyes, whereas Bob was fairly hefty and looked like a man of few words.

'Hi,' they both said casually, nodding at Shannon.

'Hi,' said Shannon.

'Well then,' said the boy, 'till next time. I know where to find you.' The three boys turned around, and only then did Shannon notice that the same symbol was sewn on to all three leather jackets: a jaguar, caught mid-leap with claws extended and jaws opened wide. The boys strolled off in the direction of the wall, and three jaguars with pointed teeth looked back at Shannon with shining, bloodthirsty eyes.

'Hey,' she suddenly called out. 'You never told me *your* name!'

The three boys stood still, then the one in the middle turned . around. 'Paul,' he said, puffing out his chest importantly. 'My name is Paul.'

The school yard was empty by the time Shannon returned to her classroom. They were doing history. But of course

Shannon couldn't concentrate on the lesson. She spent her time trying to draw a jaguar in the margin of her history book, and next to it she wrote Paul's name in jagged letters. Paul. Whoever he was, she liked him a lot, and she was already looking forward to meeting him again.

'Say, what else do you actually do? I mean *apart* from selling drugs?'

Paul sat down next to Shannon on the stone bench, smoking his joint peacefully. It was four days since their first meeting, and the boy was still wearing the same clothes.

'I stroll around the streets,' he said, 'I go to parties, amuse myself, visit friends, whatever I feel like doing.'

'Don't you go to school?'

'That was only ever trouble. The last time I went to school, I threatened the teacher with a knife, wanted to make her a little nervous. I was sent to the headmaster, and he told me I'd be expelled if it happened again. It didn't happen again, because I decided never to set foot back inside that building. I was in second grade then, I think – about seven.'

'And since then you've never been to school?'

'Never again.'

'Wow. That's cool. And what do your parents say?'

'I don't have any parents,' said Paul matter-of-factly, blowing the smoke up out of the corner of his mouth. 'My father murdered my mother when I was five. He was a drunk. He raped me a good few times until I'd had enough of it and left home. My brother and sister came with me, but the police did my brother in, and I lost track of my sister.' There was no display of emotion; he didn't bat an eyelid as he spoke. He spoke about the terrible events of his past as if it all had nothing to do with him, as if it were someone else's story, or as if it were merely a simple everyday tale.

Shannon stared at Paul dumbfounded. She didn't know what to say. She couldn't understand how Paul managed to speak of these experiences in such an open and emotionally detached manner, as if they had never had even the slightest effect on him. For Shannon, they stirred up memories of her own past. Memories of her grandfather . . . of her uncle in Los Angeles . . .

'And . . . where do you live?' she asked, attempting to hide her dismay.

'On the street,' Paul replied simply. 'We've set ourselves up in a deserted factory building, a few kilometres from the edge of town.'

'How many of you are there?'

Paul took a deep drag on his cigarette and shrugged his shoulders. 'Never counted. Most of us don't live in the factory, only the ones who really have nowhere else to go. But if we were to drum up all our members, there must be about two hundred of us. Maybe even four hundred.'

Shannon nearly fell off the bench. '*Four hundred?!!!*'

'About that. No one knows exactly. On top of that, it's always changing.'

'*Four . . . hundred?!!!*'

'All gangs have about that number of members. Didn't you know that?'

No, she didn't know that. She had no idea that there were such gangs. And she couldn't even imagine what it all meant. Four hundred people in an empty factory building? At any rate, she didn't imagine it was particularly cosy.

'Of course, there are smaller gangs,' Paul continued, 'but no one ever talks about them. The big ones rule the roost. And we're one of the big ones. At the moment, there's only one gang that's bigger than us – Rage. They're the worst, and they also have the biggest territory. But that can change quickly. We still have a score to settle there . . . Then there's the Youth Hell's Angels. They're the long-haired biker freaks. Their territory is a bit smaller, and they're also less violent. And there's Black Power, they only let blacks into their gang. Those are pretty much the most important gangs here in Cleveland.'

'Oh,' said Shannon simply, because she could think of nothing better to say to all this new information, 'and what's *your* gang called?'

'Jaguars,' said Paul, puffing out his chest.

'Jaguars,' repeated Shannon, and now she understood why Paul and the other two boys wore a jaguar on their leather jackets. 'Cool name.'

Paul nodded proudly. 'We're the best. That's why everyone wants to join. But we only take the toughest, the ones who know how to fight, you get me?'

Shannon nodded even though she didn't really know what Paul was talking about. In fact, she realised that she didn't really know much at all about life out there, life on the other side of the school wall and beyond the walls of her own home. She had never been out in the town, not only because she didn't have any friends and it was no fun alone, but also because she always had to be home on time to avoid a beating. The only thing she'd got to know in the last few months had been hostile schoolmates and the increasingly violent beatings from her father. Perhaps that was why she found Paul so attractive: he was free, could do and not do whatever he wanted, and didn't live in fear of anyone. How she wished to be like him!

'Everyone who joins our gang has our symbol tattooed on to his arm,' Paul explained. 'That's how we recognise each other. That way we know who belongs – and who doesn't.' He let his leather jacket slip down a little from one of his shoulders, so that Shannon could see the tattoo on his right upper arm. It was a bleeding heart, with 'Jaguar' written on it, and below it Shannon could see the number 666.

'What does the number mean?'

'Ever heard of the Antichrist?'

'No.'

'The Antichrist is a bit like Jesus, only the opposite.'

'What do you mean, the opposite?'

'Anti-Christ, against Christ, get it?'

'No, not a bit,' Shannon had to admit, shaking her head.

'Well, Jesus is the Son of God, and the Antichrist is the son of the devil,' Paul explained, 'and 666 is his number. One day he will rule the world, and whoever refuses to accept his number will be killed. It says it somewhere in the Bible.'

'And do you believe in that?'

'In the Bible? Definitely not. If the God in the Bible really existed, and he *really* loved his people, then why did he let my father kill my mother? Just like the police and my brother? Why didn't he step in when my father played his perverse games with me? Why? Can you answer me that?' He looked straight at Shannon. His face wore a stony hard expression, and his voice sounded reproachful. 'No, this God doesn't exist. And if he does, then I don't want to have anything to do with him. If I believe in anything, then it's the devil. And that's why we wear his sign.' He finished smoking his joint, and when the bell went he patted Shannon on the shoulder before going back to his friends.

'One day you'll make up your mind as well, trust me.'

Shannon watched him go. The jaguar on his black leather jacket stared back at her with shining eyes, as if she were the victim on which it was planning to pounce.

'Jaguars,' murmured Shannon, and she liked the sound of this name. It spoke of adventure, heroism, freedom, everything she so desperately missed in her life. The sweet scent of the hash cigarette was still hanging in the air, and Shannon wondered what it would be like to smoke it. Perhaps she should give it a go. Just to know what it was like . . .

5

Nicolas

On her way home, a few hundred metres from the school building, she heard someone calling out after her. When she turned around she saw a boy she didn't know rushing after her, as if he had something very important to tell her. She put him at about eleven years old, twelve at the most. He looked pretty harmless, was about as tall as her, slim with blond, short-cropped hair and a pale, freckled face. His schoolbooks tucked under his left arm, a guitar slung over his right shoulder, he was hurrying to catch her up. She couldn't remember having seen the boy before. But that didn't mean much. Whoever didn't hammer very hard on the little window of her space capsule didn't exist as far as she was concerned, not even if their paths had crossed a hundred times before. There were already enough ugly spectres spinning around in her head that she longed to erase from her memory. On top of that, you couldn't be expected to remember all the faces in a school with over a thousand children, and she was surprised that a boy she didn't know at all was running after her as if he had known her for ages. That had never happened to her before, and it made her curious.

'Hi,' he said, somewhat out of breath, and stretched out his hand to her, 'I'm Nicolas.'

'Hi,' growled Shannon, ignoring his hand. 'What do you want?'

'I saw you with that guy in the school yard.'

'And?'

'I wanted to warn you,' he said.

'Warn me? About what?'

'The Jaguars.'

Now Shannon was definitely curious. 'Why?'

'You shouldn't mess with them. Even the police are afraid of them.'

'How do you know that?'

'Everyone knows. Go out on the streets after midnight and see what happens. You'd have to have a death wish to voluntarily leave your home at night time. The gangs control the whole town. The Jaguars are like a pack of wolves, and woe betide the person who strays on to their patch uninvited. They kill in cold blood. They have a leader, a president, and whoever doesn't respect his orders is bumped off. But the wars are the worst of all.'

'What kind of wars?'

'The wars between the individual gangs. They fight over territory, and every time lots of people are injured and killed. Not even the police will intervene when they're beating each other's heads in. They wait until the following morning to gather up all the corpses. So you'd better give those people a pretty wide berth.'

'Hey, I'm not a baby any more,' said Shannon, although his description had made a real impression on her. 'I'm well able to look after myself, okay?'

'I just wanted to warn you. Those are dangerous friends you've chosen.'

'I'll choose my own friends, all right?' She quickened her pace in order to shake off the boy. But he stuck persistently on her heels, even though his guitar nearly slipped off his shoulder at the effort this entailed.

'Did you know that he carries a weapon?'

Shannon's ears pricked right up, but she nevertheless tried to remain as cool as possible.

'Listen here,' she said. 'No one in this school ever gave a damn about me. Up till now, Paul is the only one, the *only* one, get it? So don't you come up to me and talk about *friends*. I don't *have* any friends here, okay?'

The boy looked at her with unusual concern, and it looked as though he had something else important to get off his chest. But Shannon wouldn't let him get another word in; she turned away and crossed the road as quickly as possible.

'And as for me and Paul, that's damn all of your business, d'you hear?' She stamped off angrily, without even turning around once to look at the boy. This Nicolas had made her nervous, and not just with his information about Paul and the Jaguars. He himself had utterly thrown her, the way he spoke, the way he looked at her, the way he had followed her. Why, she kept on asking herself. Why had he done it? Why had he warned her? It needn't have bothered him a bit, not him or anybody else. Why was he sticking his nose in?

The following day as she walked along the corridor, caught up in the stream of pupils during the ten o'clock break, she saw him again. He was just coming out of the fifth-grade classroom, and at that moment he looked right at her.

'Hey, Shannon!' he called, and headed straight for her.

'There's something I forgot yesterday!' She wondered how he knew her name. He must be spying on her!

'Leave me alone, all right?' she growled.

'I thought about what you said. So I've written something down for you.' He put his hand into his pocket, pulled out a piece of paper and presented it to Shannon ceremoniously. 'Here.'

She wondered whether she should take it or simply turn around and walk away, as she had done on their first encounter. Nicolas was waiting, his hand outstretched, and his clear eyes alone seemed to encourage her to take the message. Finally she tore the note wordlessly from his hand and sank quickly back into the mass of pupils. She unfolded the paper hastily so that she could read it before Nicolas had time to catch up with her and see her reading it. The message was only two lines long, and Shannon was pretty stunned when she read it:

'Even when you think you have no friends – there is someone whose love for you knows no bounds: Jesus Christ.'

She read the message a second and then a third time, then she screwed up the note and threw it provocatively on the floor, so that Nicolas would see it when he came by. What rubbish! Jesus Christ. This Nicolas must have completely lost it. What did he know about life? Jesus Christ. And what right had he to stick his nose into her life? That was just what she needed, to meet someone who thought all her problems could be solved with one single name. Jesus Christ. It would have to be him. What did he know about love? Paul was right. The injustices he had suffered screamed out to the heavens too loudly for a loving God not to have heard them and intervened. Instead, God let it all happen, horrific and merciless, and in her own life too. And then along came this Nicolas and tried to make her buy into the idea that Jesus Christ loved her.

Most of all Shannon would have liked to hide behind the stairs and wait for the boy's expression when he found the crumpled note on the floor. But then she dismissed the idea, marched out purposefully to the school yard and looked around for Paul. She found him with Terry, behind the gym. He was taking money from a girl who quickly disappeared after the deal had been done. Bob wasn't there this time.

'Hi,' said Shannon, only now realising how much she had missed the boys – Paul in particular.

'Hi, Shannon,' said Paul, putting the cash into the pocket of his jeans. Even though he only glanced over at her and didn't even smile particularly, his curt greeting nevertheless gave her the feeling that she was accepted by him, that she belonged somehow. And that made her like him all the more.

'Where's Bob?'

'Had something urgent to do,' Paul answered vaguely. 'And you? Have you made up your mind?'

'What do you mean, made up my mind?'

'To smoke a joint with me.'

Shannon shook her head.

'Definitely not?'

Another shake of the head.

Paul reached into the inner pocket of his leather jacket, and Shannon's eyes were suddenly drawn to his hips. He was armed, Nicolas had claimed. Was that true?

Terry noticed her strangely searching look. 'What are you staring at?'

Shannon gave a barely perceptible jump. 'I'm not staring at anything.'

'Of course you are.' He turned to Paul. 'She was staring at your hips as if she was looking for something.'

'Perhaps this here?' asked Paul, and lifted up his ragged t-shirt for a split second. Shannon's jaw dropped in amazement.

Tucked fast into his tight jeans was a revolver. Shannon didn't know what to say. Of course Nicolas had said that Paul was armed, but there was a difference between simply hearing about something and actually convincing yourself of it with your very own eyes. She had never seen a weapon before in her life, apart from on TV, of course, but that didn't count. It was a weird feeling to be standing across from someone who was carrying a weapon, especially when the person in question was a twelve- or thirteen-year-old boy.

'You knew, didn't you?' said Terry.

'No, why?' contested Shannon.

'You've been finding things out about our gang, haven't you?'

'No, not on purpose . . . I mean . . .'

'They told you you'd be better off steering clear of us. Isn't that so?'

'No, I mean yes . . . I mean, it wasn't like that at all . . .'

'How wasn't it like that?' Terry continued to dig, his arms tightly folded. Shannon was confused. She didn't know whether she was better off coming out with the truth or keeping quiet. Paul gave her a friendly shove.

'It's all right, Shannon. Lots of people here know that I've got a gun. That's no big secret. I don't really care who said it to you. I just don't want you not to trust me any more because of it. You trust me, don't you?'

Shannon nodded. 'Of course I trust you.'

'I should have told you that I carry a weapon, fair enough. I hope that's not a problem for you – the gun, I mean.'

'Of course not,' Shannon muttered, embarrassed. She would have liked to ask him why he needed a weapon, but didn't dare.

'Oh, by the way,' said Paul, changing the subject abruptly and fishing a biro out of his jacket. 'If you want to meet me outside of these walls, you can get me on this number.' He took Shannon's right hand and wrote a telephone number on the back of her hand. 'Just call me and I'll come and get you, wherever you are.'

Shannon gave a mighty stare. 'You've got your own telephone?' (This was before the days when almost everyone owned a mobile phone.)

'Well, not exactly. There's a public phone right in front of the factory. You just have to ask for me.'

'And what if I get someone who doesn't know you?'

'Don't worry,' Paul answered mysteriously. 'They'll know me. All Jaguars know me.'

When Shannon left the school building that afternoon Nicholas was once again hard on her heels. This boy was certainly persistent, but what he was hoping to achieve by it was a mystery to Shannon.

'What do *you* want now?' she asked, quickening her pace.

'I wanted to know if you've read it.'

'You know what? You're getting on my nerves! Why don't you go and find yourself another victim?'

'Because God loves *you*, too.'

Shannon turned towards him in irritation. 'I'm not interested in your God! God doesn't love anyone like me, okay?'

'Jesus loves everyone, Shannon.'

'Then tell him that he doesn't need to love me.'

'Won't work.'

'Why not?'

'Because I can't stop him loving you.'

Shannon stood still and gave the boy a dirty look. 'Listen up, I don't know you, and you don't know me. So quit going on about this Jesus, and just leave me alone, get it?'

She was waiting for an answer, but Nicolas said nothing. Obviously he'd finally realised that Shannon was the wrong person for his attentions, and admitted defeat. And that was just fine by Shannon. Nobody needed to interfere in her life, at least certainly not this Nicolas with his crazy ideas. The only one who had that right was Paul. It was different with Paul. He didn't bore her with things she didn't want to hear. He only came as near to her as she allowed, and that was probably what she liked so much about him.

The friendship between Paul and Shannon grew during every ten o'clock break that Paul turned up. Paul told Shannon wild stories from his life and the life of the Jaguars. And Shannon loved diving into this world that was so foreign to her, even when there was plenty that horrified her, like the sight of Bob's badly scarred stomach from a wound an enemy had inflicted on him during a stabbing fight. The injury was also the reason why Bob hadn't shown his face in the school grounds for several weeks; when he showed Shannon the wound, sewn up with a good few stitches and almost healed, the girl felt pretty sick.

'Lucky he got me too low down,' he commented drily, 'otherwise I'd probably have kicked the bucket.'

Although the three Jaguars sometimes fed her pretty hair-raising stories, stories that almost stopped Shannon's heart simply listening to them, she grew more and more interested in the life of the gang. Perhaps this didn't really have so much to do with the pull of adventure, which hung almost tangibly in the air each time the three turned up behind the gym, nor with the call of freedom, which echoed to her from the other side of the school walls as soon as the boys had climbed back over them. Perhaps her liking for the Jaguars was based rather on a simple need to belong and feel safe. She felt in safe hands with the boys, because they seemed to understand her problems.

Paul in particular showed far more empathy with her than she had ever known from anybody else. She could simply trust him with everything. She told him about the problems with her father, the arguments with her stepmother who bullied and humiliated her. Even when her classmates ganged up on her, as was so often the case, she poured her heart out to Paul, and although he couldn't take back the mocking comments of her fellow pupils, he could at least listen to her. He listened to her, yes, he even seemed to know how she felt deep inside. He knew what she was going through, because he had gone through something similar. And that bound them.

Really it was only a question of time before Shannon couldn't handle her unhappy life any longer and did something stupid. And one morning it happened. It began in the English lesson. On that Tuesday morning they were dealing with the topic of friendship, and the teacher, a strict, fifty-year-old man with thick glasses and a suit that was always perfectly turned out and hair that was always correctly combed, set the pupils the task of describing an experience that revealed their relationship to a friend. When he called out Shannon's name she wanted to crawl right under the table, and while she desperately searched for a story to tell, the stares of her classmates bored right through her like sharpened knives. The teacher rocked impatiently in his chair and waited, his chin jutting forward, for her story.

'Well, Shannon? Have you nothing to tell us on the topic of friendship?'

'Yes, of course I have,' muttered Shannon, whereupon the first splutters in the back corner began and a boy whispered to his neighbour: 'Shannon and friendship, she'll have to cook up something good there.'

Shannon pretended she hadn't heard the remark, and began hesitantly:

'I . . . I had a close friend called Adriano, and . . .'

'That's a lie!' giggled a girl. 'She doesn't have a friend called Adriano.'

'She doesn't have a friend at all!' interjected another pupil.

'I thought it had to be a true story, Mr Thompson!'

'Or can you make up a friend if you don't have any?'

'Quiet!' The teacher banged the table with his fist, and the pupils fell momentarily silent. 'I don't want to hear any more comments like these in my lesson!' He looked at the culprits through his thick glasses and made a mental note of their names. 'You can carry on with your story, Shannon.'

Shannon had a lump in her throat. The hurtful comments from her fellow pupils made her want to cry, but she pulled herself together and swallowed her feelings. It would only have given them more reason to mock her.

'What are you going to tell?' whispered a girl behind her in her ear. 'You haven't got any friends!'

'Quiet!!!' Once again Mr Thompson banged on the desk, and this time he looked sharply at the girl behind Shannon. 'I thought I'd made myself clear, Marianne!' Marianne's name too went on his black list.

'You haven't got any friends!' repeated the girl, so softly this time that the teacher no longer heard. Just one more word, and Shannon would have turned around and punched Marianne. But she pursed her lips, curled up her fists under the table and forced herself to remain calm, even if it was difficult.

In the ten o'clock break she sat, as always, on the stone bench and twisted her dark brown hair between her fingers, staring off into empty space. When Paul arrived she was so far away that he had to call her twice before she finally reacted.

'Shannon,' said the boy, sitting down next to her, 'what's happened?'

'They showed me up,' she said weakly. 'The whole class had a great laugh. They said I haven't got any friends.'

'You know full well that's not true. You've got me, for example, a real Jaguar, member of the most feared gang in Cleveland. One word from me and a hundred Jaguars will make these cocky bigmouths wet themselves like little babies.'

A tear rolled down Shannon's cheek, and she wiped it away discreetly. Paul's words of encouragement were no comfort to her this time. She was more deeply wounded than that. Paul put his arm around her shoulder.

'Hey, girl, didn't I tell you: school here just isn't your thing. How long are you going to let it go on for? How much longer are they going to be allowed to walk all over you? Give this snobby school the finger and make up your mind at last! Make up your mind, Shannon!'

'What for? If I don't go to school any more, my father will come and beat the living daylights out of me.'

'Then give your father the finger as well! Just because he brought you into this wretched world doesn't mean you have to spend your life giving in to him! It's *your* life! Do you want to wait until he beats you to death?'

Shannon gave a deep sigh and fell silent. When the school bell rang, Paul got up, and with the words: 'You know where to find me,' he left.

Shannon was in no hurry to get to class. She knew only too well what cynical comments and looks awaited her there. But something else was waiting for her, too: on her small desk lay a folded-up piece of paper. Somebody must have put it there during break time. She unfolded the squared paper, and as soon as she had read the short message her pulse hit 180. That was just what she needed! As if she didn't have enough to put up with! She crumpled the paper hastily into her fist and marched, her mind already made up, in the direction of the door. That was too much! The final straw! She didn't have to put up with that! She bumped straight into Mr Thompson in the doorway.

'What's your rush, then?'

Shannon stormed past him, her head bowed like a bull preparing for attack, although her target wasn't a red rag but rather the door at the other end of the corridor.

'Hey!' called out her teacher in surprise. 'What's all this about, Shannon? Come back here!'

Shannon didn't take any notice of him. Her left hand was curled up into a fist, and her nostrils were flaring in anger.

'Shannon, it's time for class!'

Shannon marched on, heading straight for the fifth-grade room, and when she had reached the door she flung it open and landed right in the middle of the lesson. The teacher was standing at the blackboard, and looked at Shannon in as much amazement as the pupils.

'You should knock before you enter.'

Shannon lifted her head, cast a searching glance over the class and then headed for a blond-haired boy in the second row. And before anybody had time to react, she punched him so hard in the chest that he fell backwards while still sitting in his chair. Then she threw the crumpled note into his face, and shouted almost hysterically: 'I don't need your stupid messages, okay!'

The fifth graders sat in their places with eyes open wide in dismay, not daring to move. The teacher had dropped the chalk. She put her hand to her mouth and looked equally out of her depth. Nicolas tried to pick himself up from the floor, but Shannon was on him in a flash and began throwing punches with her fists.

'I don't want you interfering in my life! Get it?! You don't even know me! I don't want to have anything to do with you, is that clear?! I hate you! I hate you! You and your Jesus! I hate you both!'

Two boys who couldn't sit by any longer and see one of their fellow pupils being beaten up by a girl tried to tear Shannon off Nicolas – with the result that they lost their balance and joined him on the floor. A few girls circled around, a few boys began to whistle encouragingly. The pupils got up from their chairs and formed a circle around the battle scene, while the teacher stood rooted to the spot by the blackboard and called out for them to put an end to this nonsense.

Now Mr Thompson turned up in the doorway as well, and when he saw the chaos he turned right around to call the headmaster.

The boys received a few hefty kicks and punches when they tried once more to pull the maddened girl off her fellow pupil, and even when two of them held Shannon by the arms she kicked out with her legs so wildly that she knocked all the books and pens from the desks standing within reach. Only when a third boy joined in did they manage to put the ten-year-old out of action. Nicolas felt his nose carefully. It was bleeding.

'That's what you deserve!' shouted Shannon, spitting in his direction. 'That's what you're worth to me, get it? And your Jesus too! Tell the people in the church about Jesus, but not me. Not me, d'you hear?!'

Nicolas pulled himself up with effort, planted himself exhaustedly back on to the chair and wiped the blood from his nose, countering Shannon's look all the time with his bright eyes – without saying a word.

'What's all this actually about?' asked a girl quietly.

'Haven't a clue,' said another, shrugging her shoulders. 'But I don't care anyway. The main thing is, we've got out of maths.'

'I think it's to do with this note,' said a third girl, bending down to pick up the crumpled piece of paper from the floor. It was smeared with blood.

'Let's see,' said the first girl, and carefully unfolded it. The girls put their heads together while Shannon carried on cursing in the background, the teacher kept on trying to demand some sort of order, and the angry voices of Mr Thompson and the headmaster sounded in the corridor.

The message was a mere ten words long, and with the best will in the world the girls couldn't understand why these words had given rise to such chaos. It was only a few words, written with blue ink on a scrap of squared paper. Just words.

'I just want to tell you: Jesus Christ loves you!'

The girls shook their heads in disbelief.

'What rubbish.'

'Typical Nicolas.'

'And she went for him just because of that. She's crazy.' One of the girls crumpled up the scrap of paper again and threw it out of the open window. It landed somewhere on the tarmacked yard, so small and inoffensive that it was trodden to pieces by the first crowd of noisy schoolchildren who ran over it during the next break time. It was only a few words, after all. Just words.

6

The Jaguars

'Make up your mind, Shannon!' That was what Paul had said, and Shannon was becoming more and more aware of the urgency of these words. She had to make up her mind. The time was ripe . . .

After that terrible Tuesday, the headmaster had rung up Shannon's father to inform him of his daughter's violent behaviour. And Shannon's father had assured the headmaster that he would take his daughter firmly in hand – which he then did, in his own way, of course. Shannon could barely make her way to her bed, so strong a hand had her father taken, and she cried the whole night long out of anger, despair and a sense of endless loneliness. She felt as if the whole world had taken oath against her, and there was nobody there who would defend her cause. Nobody at all.

And then, on a Saturday afternoon in the middle of June 1982, she made up her mind. It began when she inadvertently woke her father from his precious afternoon nap with the noise of the vacuum cleaner; since her father had only just got back from a prolonged business trip and was therefore fairly tired, this disturbance had deadly consequences. Foaming with rage, he appeared in the sitting room, hurled Shannon around the whole room by the hair, boxed her repeatedly around the ears and then began beating her head against the wall. Shannon screamed and begged him to stop, tears streaming down her face. But her father took no notice of her, instead reprimanding and swearing at her because his sleep had been disturbed; each time he bashed her head against the wall, it resounded throughout the whole house. Even Valerie appeared out of the dining room to ask what Shannon had done this time, but then withdrew with the comment 'Typical Shannon!' and left the ten-year-old girl to her fate. Shannon screamed like a pig on a spit.

'Stop it, Dad! Stop it!' she cried desperately, upon which her father grabbed her by the throat with his right hand so that she could barely breathe. He pressed her hard against the wall and looked at her menacingly with his big round eyes.

'If you don't stop this whingeing right now,' he hissed, so close to her face that she could feel the heat of his breath, 'I'll kill you!'

Shannon froze. She had always been afraid of her father, but never quite as much as now. She didn't make a sound. Her sobs died away. Her father dropped her like a doll, and Shannon sank to the floor shaking and gasping for air like a fish out of water. She watched her father climb up the stairs to the first floor. She was suddenly desperately afraid that he would interpret her breathless panting as quiet sobbing and would turn around all of a sudden and beat her head for so long against the wall that it would kill her. She believed he was capable of it. Her father was capable of anything, even that.

She covered her mouth with her hand to stifle the tears. Her limbs were shaking with fear. Her head was pounding as if an army of a thousand woodpeckers were at work inside it, and she felt as if her skull was about to split at any moment. *If you don't stop this whingeing right now, I'll kill you!* Her father's words echoed in her head, forcing her to swallow down every last whimper.

Just don't cry now, she thought, just don't do that. She mustn't cry. Not in her room, not secretly in the toilet. Her father mustn't see her crying any more – not today, not tomorrow, not even in a week's time. And he wasn't the only one: no one must see her crying any more. No one must ever see a tear on her face – this was what she swore to herself at that moment, and she was determined to keep her oath, no matter what happened. She would keep her composure, she would grit her teeth, she would be brave, she would even keep going when it no longer seemed possible. Yes, that was what she would do. She would never cry again, never ever! Her whole life long!

Never ever.

She wiped her wet eyes, swallowed down the lump in her throat and all of a sudden felt strangely strong. And, driven on by this sudden surge of rebellion, she knew in that very moment that the time had come for her to make up her mind.

The time was ripe.

Over-ripe.

She went up to her room, locked the door from inside, sat on her bed and waited. A quarter of an hour, perhaps half an hour, in any case long enough to assume that her father had fallen asleep again and would not hear her. Her stepmother was going about her own business and wouldn't hear her either. They wouldn't suspect anything until they came to check on little Melissa and found the door locked. And by the time they had found a replacement key or broken down the door, Shannon would be long gone.

She cast a glance at her half-sister, almost two years old now, sitting happily on the floor playing with building bricks. Would Dad hit her too when she was older? Shannon sat down next to her and pressed a big kiss on to her fat little cheek. Melissa looked up at her innocently with wide eyes, and then turned her attentions back to her bricks. Shannon took her money box out of the cupboard, emptied the few coins on to the bed and put them into her trouser pocket. Then she slipped on her trainers, tied her denim jacket around her waist and went to the window. With one final look she made sure that she hadn't forgotten anything, opened the window and sat on the window sill. The garage roof was less than two metres below her. She turned herself around, curled her fingers around the sill and held on tightly until she could feel the tin roof under her feet. Noiselessly as a cat she glided over the roof and chose a suitable spot to jump down to the ground. Then she crept along the wall until she had reached the corner of the house. Having made certain her stepmother wasn't by chance standing at one of the windows from which she could be seen, she then ran down the narrow path to the gate, from the gate to the street, and along the street to the main road, Mayfield Avenue. Panting for breath, she stood there for a moment, glanced over her shoulder a second time to make sure that no one had followed her, and then walked the final 500 metres to the nearest public telephone at a slightly easier pace.

'Just call me and I'll come and get you, wherever you are,' Paul had said. Shannon pulled a few coins from her pocket and dialled his number, which she had long since learned by heart in case she should one day have urgent need of it. And now she needed it, very urgently – in fact, so urgently that her fingers shook slightly as she dialled. Paul was her only hope. She didn't know who else she could have turned to. She didn't have anybody else. Her heart was beating fit to burst as she waited for someone to answer. She let it ring at least fifteen times, and with each pause she grew more nervous. What if it was the wrong number? What if Paul wasn't there?

At long last there was action at the other end, and a sleepy male voice answered. 'Yes?'

'I . . . I'd like to speak to Paul.' There was a short pause, and Shannon began to wonder if the connection was faulty.

'Hello?'

The line crackled in the receiver.

'And *who* wants to speak to Paul?' said the voice, sounding tired.

'Shannon.'

'Does he know you?'

'Yes, from school. He told me I could ring him whenever . . .'

'Just a moment.' There was a crackling sound again, and Shannon could hear a few fuzzy voices in the background. She checked to see how much credit she had left and fingered her other coin. It seemed like an eternity before the voice returned.

'Hang on.'

She shifted impatiently from one foot to the other and waited. Just to be sure, she inserted the second coin. And then, at long last, he came to the phone.

'Paul.'

At the mere sound of his voice she began to breathe more easily.

'Paul,' she said in relief, 'It's me, Shannon. I've run away from home.'

'Where are you?'

'In Mayfield Avenue, in front of McDonald's. Could you . . . could you come and get me?'

'Of course. Wait for me. I'm on my way.'

'Thanks, Paul.' The other end went dead, and Shannon

replaced the receiver. Then she sat down on the low wall in front of the fast food restaurant and waited.

Just how long she sat there and waited she couldn't say. It must have been hours, because dusk began to fall and Shannon was still sitting on the same wall. Had Paul forgotten her? Unlikely. He had said she was to wait for him. So she would wait, because he would come, she knew he would.

A police car drove past her twice, and on each occasion it made her jump slightly, out of fear that her father had already noticed her absence and notified the police. But perhaps he hadn't called the police at all. Perhaps he was quite happy that she'd run away. Perhaps he thought he needn't bother the police, because she would soon return home anyway, tail between her legs, full of remorse. But she would never return, never again. She wouldn't let her father beat her like a dog any more, never again. She had made up her mind, and there was no way back.

Whatever happened, it would be better than going back home – of this she was convinced. But she wasn't entirely happy with her present situation either. What was waiting for her? The unknown tormented her. Thousands of different and opposing thoughts shot through her head as she sat on the low wall in front of McDonald's and waited for Paul. Even though nothing would have made her turn back now, she nevertheless had the peculiar impression that she had lost part of herself. However bad her home had been, it had been her one security, and exchanging this for a piece of street frightened her. A lot. How would she, a ten-year-old girl, survive on the streets of Cleveland? What would become of her?

Terrible feelings coursed through her chest. She felt as if she were sitting in a bottomless black hole and she was slowly beginning to dissolve and trickle out into nothing at all. Really, she wanted to cry her eyes out – but no, she had promised herself never to cry again. She was torn in two. A battle was raging in her heart, a battle which she would lose either way. She sat on the low wall as if she were in a trance, inwardly battling against her own feelings and outwardly staring stupidly ahead, not taking any notice of the people and traffic passing by.

Suddenly he appeared in front of her. She hadn't seen him coming. He was suddenly just standing there, his legs wide apart like in a western, his hands on his hips, his cigarette hanging from the corner of his mouth. He was absolutely silent.

'Paul,' murmured Shannon, relieved. Surprising even herself, she jumped up and hugged the boy spontaneously. He barely reacted, remained fairly stiff and looked her up and down sarcastically, as if he had long since known that it would come to this.

'Get on,' he ordered unemotionally, and pointed to his motorbike. She was surprised that he didn't ask her a single question, didn't make a single comment, didn't offer a single word of comfort. He seemed strangely cold and distant, completely different from how she had otherwise experienced him. But perhaps she was just imagining it. In any case, she was happy that she was finally on her way, and she sat up behind him on the motorbike, put her arms around his body, and together they set off.

It was a long journey across the entire town, and as they thundered past grey house after grey house and got nearer and nearer to the edge of town, Shannon became increasingly uncomfortable. Where on earth were they going? The sun was already below the horizon and a dusky grey was stretched out above their heads. After about forty minutes Paul finally slowed down and pointed to the base of a low chain of hills.

'It's over there, between the pine trees.' A huge building emerged out of the darkness. It looked like an abandoned storehouse or an empty factory. Large parts of the walls were a rusty black, probably the result of a fire, and a third of the roof was entirely destroyed. Most of the narrow windows, all at least four metres high, were also broken and looked like caves carved out in a cliff. The complex nestled eerily among the trees, like the backdrop to a horror film. So this was the famous hideout of the Jaguars, thought Shannon, and shivered.

Paul left his motorbike on the grassy ground next to some other motorbikes and nodded to Shannon to follow him. The place was littered with charred bits of machinery, broken glass, pieces of wood, metal poles and a lot of rubbish. From inside the building came muffled voices, laughter and music.

As they approached the rusty entrance Shannon's feet grew heavier and heavier. She was afraid of this meeting with the Jaguars. She was afraid of the president and his power. Most of all, she was afraid of what was waiting for her behind those black walls.

'Hey, cheer up!' said Paul encouragingly. 'They won't eat you.'

'And what if they don't accept me?'

'You don't need to worry about anything when you're with me, girl,' Paul said importantly, and took her arm. He pushed the door open a crack and pulled Shannon in behind him into the hall, the Jaguars' quarters. It took a while for her eyes to get used to the darkness. The room was sparsely lit by candles and the light from the occasional camp fire, around which small groups of people were gathered. Shannon was hit by the penetratingly sweet aroma of hashish mixed with cigarette smoke and the smell of alcohol. Someone somewhere right at the back of the building was playing the guitar. The squawking sound of music from a transistor radio was coming from another corner. A few dark figures stood wrapped around each other right next to the entrance, although it was impossible to tell whether they were male or female. Less than ten metres away, a boy lay quaking on the ground, making strange noises. Another boy reeled past, without taking the slightest bit of notice of him. He had a bottle in his hand and put it to his mouth and drank greedily, slopping half of the liquid over his chin and neck as he did so. A few boys and girls were sitting right next to him, passing a cigarette round in a circle. And further away, a couple were moaning with pleasure under a woollen blanket.

Shannon felt as if she were in some sort of crazy dream. She had never seen the like of it in her life before. All around her were kids blatantly and shamelessly filling their time with drugs and sex. Shannon was disgusted by it, but even this repulsive orgy seemed better than the madness back home. Everything was better than her home, even hell itself.

And then something happened which completely took Shannon's breath away: Paul opened the popper fastenings on his leather jacket, and at the mere sound of the poppers opening an incredible silence fell over the whole place, as if to some invisible command, and everyone looked in his direction. Everyone. As if the president in person had deigned to enter. So was Paul . . . ? Shannon's jaw dropped in amazement.

'Don't let me disturb you, guys,' said Paul, and his voice echoed through the factory building, 'I've just brought a girl with me.'

'For us or for you?' called someone from the crowd.

'Hey,' replied Paul, pointing with his index finger to the boy in question. 'Hands off, okay?'

'But of course,' was the good-humoured reply. 'I wouldn't make the mistake of touching the president's girl.'

'I'd certainly advise you not to!'

Shannon couldn't believe it. Paul was actually the president of the Jaguars. She had made friends with the very president of the Jaguars himself! Without realising it. The boss of the most feared gang in Cleveland. In person. That was something, really something!

The din returned to its former level, and Paul turned to Shannon. 'Didn't I tell you, as long as you're with me, nothing can happen to you?'

'Why didn't you tell me that you . . . ?'

'I didn't want to frighten you.'

'Crazy. You're really the president of the Jaguars?'

'You'd better believe it.'

'Why *you* in particular?'

'Because I'm the best.' He patted Shannon on the shoulder. 'If you want to be president, it's not your age or your muscles that are most important, but this here.' He tapped his temple with his index finger. 'With this you can achieve anything you want. Anything.' He took her by the arm. 'Come on, let me introduce you to a few of the more important people.'

They crossed the room and headed for a group of kids who were standing in the semi-darkness over by the right-hand wall, chatting excitedly. They were smoking cigarettes and drinking out of a bottle which they continually passed from one to another. A nearby fire danced light over their figures. When Paul appeared with Shannon, they stopped talking.

'Guys, this is Shannon,' said Paul without further ado. 'Shannon, these are the heads of our gang. Edmond.' A huge boy offered Shannon the hardened paw of a workman, and when he squeezed her hand she thought he was going to break all her fingers. His skin was coffee brown, his black hair consisted of hundreds of little plaits gathered together at the nape of his neck with a cloth; his woollen cap was crowned by a black pair of shades with small, round lenses.

'Edmond is our war minister,' explained Paul. 'He arranges with other gangs when, where and with what weapons we'll have our next battle. We call him Elephant, by the way, not because of his size, but because of his memory. He never forgets anybody who's had the better of him. He's always got some old scores to settle with people who provoked him years ago. And when Edmond draws his gun, you're best off steering well clear of him.'

Paul put his hand on the shoulder of a strong-looking boy of medium height. 'This is Johnny – the Apache, as we call him.'

This Johnny actually really did have the angular facial features of an Indian, together with brown watchful eyes, long black hair, and the athletic body of a footballer to boot.

'Johnny is our contact man for the drugs trade,' Paul explained. 'All of the Jaguars' drugs trade goes through him. He deals with the drug barons in Cleveland and has contacts with the dealers in Detroit, New York and other cities. He's one of our gang's best fighters. He claims that one of his great-grandfathers was an Apache warrior. That's where the name comes from. Anyhow, Johnny sure knows how to use a knife. That's a fact. And so it's better not to annoy him.'

He turned to the third boy, a rather scrawny lad with blond, tangled hair. Only now did Shannon recognise him. It was Terry.

'Welcome to the Jaguars,' he said, pressing her hand. 'Was about time you joined us.'

'Terry is our vice-president,' said Paul. 'Looks more harmless than he really is. When he's high, he could strangle a lion with his bare hands, I'd put money on it.' He pointed vaguely into the darkness. 'And you'll get to know the others in time. There's Rick, for example, who always knows where to palm off stolen motorbikes and cars. And then there are numerous smaller gangs of twenty to forty members within the Jaguars, each with their own leader. And these in turn are under my command. Before a battle, we first of all discuss the battle plan with the group leaders, then they drum up their groups, relay the most important information, and eventually we go to war. Everything's excellently organised, everyone knows what they've got to do. That's the way it works, Shannon. That's us, the Jaguars, the terrifying, invincible Jaguars.'

He took the bottle from Terry's hand, drank a deep swig from it, wiped his mouth with the back of his hand and passed the bottle on to Shannon. She hesitated. The pungent smell of the indefinable drink was alone enough to make her eyes water. Whatever it was, it was definitely strong enough to blow up a cliff-face should you hold a match to the mouth of the bottle.

'Hey, you're with the Jaguars here! If that little drink's too much for you, then you're better off going back home!' said a grinning black girl. She had suddenly appeared out of the darkness and had immediately begun weaving her way around Edmond like a cat looking for food.

Shannon knew that she was going to have to drink the strong stuff if she wanted to belong and not be mocked as a weakling. So she gathered up her courage, put the bottle to her mouth and took an extra long swig. The liquid burned in her throat like fire, and she would have most liked to spit the booze right back out again.

'Wicked, eh?' said Paul, and then gave her a cigarette which he had 'borrowed' from Johnny. Shannon knew that she was being tested. This was probably how every newcomer was greeted, and whoever didn't prove that all that stuff had no effect on them was a pathetic loser, unsuitable for a gang like the Jaguars. She watched a boy some distance away as he sucked at the last tiny bit of a hash cigarette, burning both fingers and lips as he did so but apparently not even noticing. And when the butt had shrunk down to the last few millimetres he simply stuck it straight into his mouth and ate it.

Shannon stared at the cigarette between her fingers and swallowed. More and more onlookers came by, curious to see how she would cope with the ceremonial initiation rites. If she flunked it now, she would have missed her chance, irretrievably so. She would have to go for broke – there wasn't going to be another opportunity. Slowly she brought the cigarette to her lips and took the first drag. It resulted in a pitiful coughing fit, and the onlookers laughed and called her a weakling. She felt sick as a dog, and she was afraid that she would have to throw up if she took a second drag. But the jeers from the youths spurred her on. After the third drag she felt better, and Paul exchanged the cigarette for one of his own hand-rolled ones.

'Well, what do you think? *Now* will you smoke a joint with me?'

'Have you got a light?' asked Shannon in reply. Paul smiled and lit up the hash cigarette with his lighter. She took a deep drag and sucked the narcotic smoke down into her lungs, as Paul had explained to her and shown her on many occasions at school. She soon felt dizzy. But immediately afterwards she began to feel a strange but very pleasing feeling taking over. It was as if she were diving into another world, a world some-where over the clouds, a world in which everyone was weight-less, a world in which the impossible was suddenly attainable.

A girl came up to her, took the joint out of her hand and in so doing touched her fingers, as if by accident.

'I'm Jeanette,' she said by way of introduction, gave her a wink and took a deep drag from the cigarette, so that her cheeks hollowed in as she sucked. She was tall and slim and had very short blond hair. With her left thumb casually stuck into her tight jeans, her over-large checked shirt hanging carelessly over it, and the joint in her right hand, she looked like some sort of macho out of a cigarette advertisement.

'Watch out, she's got the hots for you!' somebody called out at that moment, but before Shannon had time to realise what was going on Jeanette pulled her to her, gave her a passionate kiss, and in so doing blew the sweet smoke from the hash cigarette into her mouth. No one seemed to find this in the least disturbing, and if Paul hadn't intervened, Jeanette would definitely have carried right on.

'Hey,' he said, pushing in between the two girls, 'Shannon's already taken, in case you hadn't realised!'

'I'm not jealous,' replied Jeanette, and gave Shannon another wink. 'But should you change your mind . . .'

'That's enough,' said Paul, and pulled Shannon in behind him. 'Leave her alone!'

'Spoilsport,' said Jeanette sulkily, blowing her smoke into his face and turning away.

'Hey, Paul,' piped up Johnny the Apache, 'how's about some coke? I got a big delivery just yesterday.'

'Good quality?'

'The finest.'

'Let's go into my office, we won't be disturbed quite as much there.'

Paul's 'office' was a bare room at the other end of the hall. There were several empty rooms there, which probably really had once been offices. In actual fact, they were containers assembled from prefabricated parts, as you might find on building sites or at fairs, and here too the fire had left its trace. Everything was rusty black and partly dilapidated. There was a table and several chairs in Paul's office, as well as a cut-up old sofa and a mattress in an equally ragged state with a grey woollen cover.

There were six of them there: Paul, Terry, Johnny, Edmond with his girl and Shannon. Johnny emptied a white powder on to a piece of mirror-glass, which he had found on the way and polished clean on his trousers. Although she was still feeling foggy from her first hashish cigarette, Shannon understood that the fine powder wasn't simple flour, but rather cocaine. With the edge of a piece of paper Johnny divided the few grams into six equal portions, and then each of them snorted the powder into their noses through a fine straw. Shannon took part in the whole procedure without a second thought.

The effect was apparent in just a few minutes. Suddenly Shannon was wide awake and filled with an inexplicable sense of power. She felt capable of anything. She would even have had the courage to stand up and address all of the Jaguars, or to stand up to her classmates. She wouldn't even have taken fright at the thought of spitting into her father's face. She believed herself capable of anything, literally anything. She wasn't the little, unimportant Shannon any more. Never before in her life had she been so fearless and uninhibited. She was no longer herself. She was blown away by it.

Paul began to hug and kiss her. She let it happen. They lay down on the mattress next to the sofa and forgot time and place. When Paul first penetrated her she thought involuntarily of her grandfather and her uncle, but somehow she managed to suppress those terrible memories. That was the past. And that was what it should remain. From now on, this was the beginning of something new. From now on she was with the Jaguars.

7

Survive!

'Hey, Shannon! Me and Johnny are going to New York today. Want to come along?' Paul was standing in front of her, feet planted squarely on the ground. It was morning. Shannon rubbed her eyes sleepily, stretched and sat up. She had a pounding headache and felt pretty lousy. All she could remember of the previous night was having to throw up on several occasions.

'Why New York?'

'Johnny's got a deal to do there. And I fancy a little trip.'

'Isn't that a bit far?'

'Just six hundred kilometres. If we give it some gas, we'll be there by tonight. Otherwise tomorrow. Fancy it?'

Of course she fancied it. She had never been to New York. And exploring this world-famous city with Paul would be anything other than boring. Her headache would sort itself out at some stage.

An hour later, they set off. Shannon travelled with Paul; Johnny had his own motorbike. They didn't take any luggage, apart from a big empty bag, a few joints and a few grams of cocaine.

'We'll get the rest on the way,' Paul said. 'The world belongs to *us*!'

After several hours, they stopped at a petrol station with a service shop. Johnny instructed the petrol attendant to fill both motorbikes, and Paul slung the big bag over his shoulder and signalled to Shannon to follow him in to do some shopping.

A bell rang when they entered the small shop. An overweight woman with an unhealthy, pallid face and a double chin was sitting behind the counter, flicking through a fashion magazine and chewing on some gum. She glanced up when the two came in, and then immediately returned to her reading. They were the only customers in the run-down shop. A dusty old ventilator hung in the corner. There was a telephone on one of the walls which looked as if it dated back to the nineteenth century. A large kitchen clock hung over the glass entrance door; it was running two hours slow.

'Take whatever you want,' said Paul in a low voice as they walked along the aisles, 'everything's free today.' They stuffed the bag full with food until it was almost bursting at the seams. Then Paul walked cool as a cucumber past the counter and towards the exit. Shannon trailed after him with an uneasy feeling in her stomach. She had known all along that Paul had no intention of paying for the food. But what if the woman at the counter smelled a rat?

No sooner had the thought suggested itself to Shannon than the woman cried out. 'Hey! You! Wait!'

Paul turned around innocently. 'Are you speaking to me?'

'Who else? What have you got in that bag?'

'You surely don't think that we've stolen something?'

The woman put her magazine to one side and motioned to him to come over. 'Come here, my boy. I'd like to have a look in that bag of yours.'

'Okay, lady,' said Paul, and lay the bag on the broken black conveyor belt. He reached under his shirt, and before the cashier had managed to look inside the bag he was holding his gun under her nose. The woman turned ghostly pale, even paler than she normally was.

'Well,' said Paul, 'about time that this dusty old hole saw a bit of life, don't you think?'

'Please . . . don't hurt me!' pleaded the woman. She glanced fleetingly out at the petrol attendant, the only person who could have come to her help in this deserted area. But he was engrossed in conversation with Johnny and had his back turned to them.

Paul seemed to read her thoughts. 'My partner is armed too, by the way,' he warned. 'So no funny games. We blasted someone for just a few coins before.' He nodded to Shannon. 'Cut the phone line in two. I don't want her to set the police on our heels when we're done.'

Shannon did what he demanded, and the woman became increasingly nervous, although she didn't dare make a sound. Paul clearly felt at ease in his role.

'While we're at it, open the till. Come on!' The woman obeyed, her hands shaking. 'And now put it all in a plastic bag. The notes first.' He watched all of her movements, clearly enjoying watching his victim sweat.

'Give it here,' he said, and tore the bag and its contents from her hand. 'And now, close your eyes.' The cashier was shaking all over.

'Please . . . please don't kill me! Please . . . !'

'Eyes closed, I said!' She obeyed, quaking with fear, and Paul turned his weapon around and walloped her on the head with the handle. The woman collapsed behind the counter, and Paul put the revolver back in his trousers.

'Let's go,' he said, throwing the bag over his shoulder and passing the bag with the money to Shannon. 'Child's play, see? Take note for next time.'

Once outside, Paul gave a sign to the Apache, who nodded in response. 'Here come my friends,' he said, and turned towards them. 'Hey, guys, we still owe the man $30 for the petrol.'

'Our cashier will take care of that,' said Paul, giving Shannon a meaningful look. She understood, gathered the correct amount from the bag and passed it to the pump attendant, avoiding his eyes.

His gaze wandered from the plastic bag to Shannon, from Shannon to Paul and the bulging bag he carried over his shoulder, and suddenly he asked: 'Can I offer you an ice cream?'

Paul was immediately suspicious.

'Why?'

'Well,' explained the man, 'we've got a few ice creams that have gone past their sell-by date and . . .'

'Know what, mister?' said Paul, spitting on the ground. 'I think you're trying to take the mickey. There's no freezer in your shop.'

'It's in the room next door,' assured the pump attendant, and smiled. 'We've got vanilla, chocolate, strawberry . . .'

'Rubbish,' interrupted Johnny, and in one quick movement he pulled out his gun. 'You weren't perhaps hoping to call the police?'

The man froze. 'Me? Call . . . why?'

Paul too pulled out his weapon from under his shirt, and while Johnny slowly slunk around the man like a wild animal, Paul held his gaze, his eyes narrowed to slits.

'We're no novices, not like you, Grandpa. The phone line is cut, Fatty in the shop is unconscious on the floor and seeing as you wanted to try and pull a fast one on us, we should do you in right here and now.'

The panic in the man's eyes was evident. But he didn't make a sound.

'Is that your car over there?' Paul nodded to an old Land Rover standing about ten metres away under a lone tree.

The man stood there as if paralysed, and still couldn't manage a single sound.

'Theoretically speaking, you could drive into the next village in that and sound the alarm.' He pointed his weapon at the vehicle's tyres and gave two well-aimed shots. 'Well, not any more you can't. And just to be sure . . .' He nodded to Johnny who struck from behind with the handle of his gun. The petrol attendant sank noiselessly to the ground.

Johnny's facial expression stayed just as cold and hard as it had been up to now, and he asked: 'Shall I finish him off?'

'Leave him,' Paul decided generously. 'Just take the $30 from him, and we'll be off.'

Johnny tucked away the money and kicked the man to one side with his pointed cowboy boots.

Paul winked at Shannon, who had watched helplessly from the sidelines.

'Lesson number one: whoever encounters a Jaguar should remember it for the rest of his life. Take note of that, Shannon.'

They reached New York that same evening, shortly before midnight. Paul decided to look up a few friends, who lived in a rather shady area of town and also belonged to a gang. The loud noise of their motorbikes was almost ghostly as it echoed through the dead streets. Only the muted thumping of disco music sounded from the late-licence pubs, in front of which a few half-drunk men lounged around with scantily clad girls on their arms. They turned off into a side street, and under a fire-escape ladder in a back yard they found the entrance to a large, sparsely lit room. The atmosphere was the same as in the Jaguars' hideout: cold and tense. Drugs, sex and alcohol seemed to play an equally decisive role in the lives of the kids here, gathered as they were in the underground rooms. Paul asked after his friends and found them in a corner, sitting on the floor smoking hashish cigarettes; in the centre of their circle were a couple of half-empty whisky and vodka bottles which they passed around every now and again. Paul, Johnny and Shannon joined them and amused themselves well into the early hours, drinking and smoking joints; they didn't settle down to sleep until the sun was beginning to rise the following morning.

Shannon woke up sometime near midday, and was amazed to discover that she had slept on the bare floor. Bottles, cigarette stubbs and even a few used needles lay all over the place. Various youths were also sleeping on the ground, as if they had been tipped out of a wheelbarrow and then simply lay where they fell. One boy lay face down in his own vomit. Strangely enough, Shannon was no longer disgusted by it. Her eyes already seemed to have got used to such sights.

An hour later, Shannon and Paul set off to explore New York. Johnny had other plans, and they agreed to meet up again back in their friends' hideout the following morning at the very latest. It was a fantastic day. They went to McDonald's twice, and Paul bought Shannon a black leather jacket like all the Jaguars had, and tight jeans and steel-capped boots to go with it. To top it all off, Shannon had a punk hair-cut done in a hair salon: a red mohican, blue sides shaved down to the last few millimetres, and a long green rat's tail. She was delighted with it.

'Well, what do you think?'

Paul looked her up and down with folded arms.

'Perfect disguise. Even if your picture is hanging in every police station, nobody would figure that *you're* the missing girl.'

'That's what I hope. If the police find me and take me back to my father . . .' She left the rest of the thought unspoken. 'My father isn't human. You can't even begin to imagine.'

'Oh yes I can, Shannon. I know very well what you're talking about. Or have you forgotten what *my* father did to me?'

No, Shannon had not. She knew his story and how similar it was to hers.

'Did you ever wish your father was dead?' she asked him suddenly.

'Thousands of times,' answered Paul. 'And I'll show you what I do when that happens. Come with me.'

They travelled along a maze of streets until on a building site Paul found what he was looking for: an iron bar. He picked up the bar from the ground, weighed it in his hand and nodded to Shannon.

'And now, watch.' He went up to a parked car, stood next to it with his legs planted firmly on the ground, and with a terrifying war-whoop he brought the iron bar crashing down on to the windscreen. It broke on the third strike.

'Now you,' said Paul, and passed the heavy metal bar to Shannon. 'You'll see just how much good it does you.'

Shannon chose the rear windscreen, grabbed hold of the bar with both hands, pursed her lips, raised the bar above her head and struck. Nothing happened.

'You have to think of your father. Imagine the car is your father. Imagine you're punching his face in and paying him back for everything he's done to you. Hit him, go on!'

Shannon struck again, this time with twice as much rage, and the windscreen splintered just as ice breaks when you stand on it.

'Yeah! Just like that! Hit him! And scream! Let out your hatred! Scream! Hit! Finish him off!'

Shannon swung the bar above her head, let out a scream and brought the bar crashing down. There was a splintering, splitting sound, and with another blow the windscreen had broken into a thousand pieces.

'More! Again! Give it to him! He's earned it!'

Now Shannon really got going. She attacked the remaining windows, and with each blow she became wilder. It really was as if she was letting out all her hatred, the humiliation and the frustration that had been building up in her over all those years, letting it all out on the car – it was an incredible feeling of release. Paul found himself a second iron bar and joined in the destruction. People appeared at the windows and held their hands in front of their mouths in dismay. Curious onlookers stood a safe distance away, not daring to join in.

'Why doesn't somebody call the police? Call the police!' someone eventually shouted. The cry came from one of the windows on the second floor of the building on the other side of the street.

'Shut your mouth, Grandma!' Paul shouted up to the woman. Shannon had already singled out a second vehicle, and Paul was starting on his third.

'Stop that, you brats!' shouted the same woman. 'It's a disgrace! You should be locked up for this!'

'Mind your own damn business!' Shannon snarled at the tiresome woman, stepping out into the middle of the street and slinging the bar furiously in the direction of the window. The woman managed to duck out of the way just in the nick of time, then there was a smashing sound as the window pane shattered.

'Wow!' said Paul, impressed. 'Good aim.'

'That'll teach her,' Shannon growled, and even though the

woman didn't dare to put her head out of the window again, Shannon roared up at her in rage, shaking her fist: 'Whoever takes on the Jaguars will remember it for the rest of their life! Just you take note of that!'

The audience began to swell. Paul took his bar and threw it in their direction, scattering them every which way.

'Come on, Shannon, time to split.' They got back on to the motorbike, and Paul gave it some.

'Rule number two,' he said as they sped away, 'a Jaguar never lets himself get caught.'

Shannon clung on to Paul, and felt absolutely content. She had never known someone like Paul, someone who took her seriously and managed to make such light work of teaching her everything she needed to know in order to survive on the streets. On top of that, he was fearless, street-wise and adventurous into the bargain, and Shannon liked him all the more for it. She would never have believed that Paul would let her down one day. But that was just what he did, not even two weeks after they had returned from New York to Cleveland. And it was one of the worst moments of her whole life . . .

'Hey, Shannon, I've a question.'

Shannon was sitting on the ground with Rick, smoking a cigarette, when Paul joined them.

'Sit yourself down,' said Rick, and moved a little to one side. Paul sat down and turned once more to Shannon.

'You've already been with us for two weeks, and I think it's time for you to think about whether you want to stay. I mean, for ever.'

'Of course I want to,' answered Shannon. 'Where else have I got?'

'The thing is: whoever wants to become part of our gang has to take part in a ritual.'

'Ritual?'

'It's like a test of your courage. If you pass it, you're one of us, a Jaguar. Is that what you want?'

'Of course, Paul! You know that's what I want.'

'That means you swear eternal faith and submission to the gang. Your life belongs to the Jaguars. If the gang goes to war, you go with them. Your enemies are our enemies, and our enemies are your enemies. We will protect you, as long as you don't do anything to put our gang in danger. We are one, solidarity until death do us part. Is that what you want?'

Shannon nodded, resolutely. 'And what if I *don't* pass this test of courage?'

Paul hesitated. 'You have to pass it,' he said mysteriously.

The entrance ritual was set for a Friday. Apart from Shannon, there was a second girl taking part. She had been with the gang for a little longer than Shannon, and had long blonde hair, green-grey eyes and a little snub nose. She was also ten years old, and was called Patricia.

Neither Patricia nor Shannon could guess what lay ahead of them. Paul only answered their questions about what form the test would take with the remark: 'You'll find out when it's time.' They couldn't get anything else out of him. The tension hung over them like a guillotine.

On the Friday evening Paul and Terry led the two girls to two empty rooms at the back of the hall. There was a small table in each of the rooms, and on the table lay plentiful amounts of heroin and cocaine, along with all the equipment necessary to snort or inject the drugs. That was all.

'You'll find out about the second part of the test when I let you out again,' said Paul, and pushed each girl into a room.

'And how long are we going to stay in here?' asked Shannon.

'Three days.'

'Three days?! Do we at least get something to eat or drink?'

'You've got everything that you need. Have fun. The test has already begun.' With that, Paul closed one of the doors, Terry the other, and the girls were left to their own devices.

Shannon stared, rather perplexed, at the locked door and then at the table with the drugs, before finally settling herself down in a corner on the ground. Locked up for three days with no food or water, that wasn't the nicest of things to look forward to. At least they had enough drugs to help pass the time. But what was it all about? What was the snag? Spending three days in a locked room didn't really demand much bravery. That alone was no test of your courage. So what did Paul intend by it? What would be waiting for her at the other side of the door when she was allowed back out in three days' time?

For the first two hours, Shannon did nothing; she simply sat there and stared off into space. But then she couldn't resist the need any longer, and snorted a first small portion of cocaine. After that followed three days and three nights of a drug-induced haze, and when Paul opened the door of her cell on Monday evening, Shannon had mutated under the strong influence of the drugs into a heap of utter misery. Paul waved her out, and as she stood in the doorway he put a knife into her hand.

'Survive!' was all he said to her. Then he gave her a soft kick, and she stumbled into the murky factory hall, not in the least understanding what was going on. The audience that had gathered for the spectacle opened up a narrow alleyway to let her through, and there, a few metres away from her, in the middle of a marked-out circle, stood Patricia – also with a knife in her hand. Patricia was snorting like a bull preparing to charge, and Shannon felt as though her blood was going to freeze in her veins. So *that* was what Paul had thought up: a battle to the death! That was the test of courage! Whoever survived could stay in the gang!

The audience whistled and clapped, stamped on the ground with their feet and shouted their names in turn. Many hands pushed Shannon into the battle arena. The air seemed to be buzzing above their heads.

'Go on,' she heard somebody near her shout, 'tear her to bits!'

'We want to see blood!' shouted another.

'Finish her off.'

Shannon gripped her knife and made a step towards Patricia. She automatically dropped into a defence position, her knife pointing at Shannon. They prowled around one another like wild cats, circling around, bent low to the ground, the deadly weapon held out in front, each girl holding back and registering every movement her opponent made.

Shannon was the first to attack. She rushed forward and tripped up Patricia, who fell to the floor, lunging out with her knife as she did so. Shannon kicked her in the stomach with her pointed boots and also struck out with her knife. She injured the girl's shoulder. But before she could stab for a second time her opponent rolled on to her side, lifted herself in a flash from the floor and stabbed Shannon's left arm. Shannon screamed. The crowd roared in excitement. The sight of blood flowing drove them wild, like piranhas.

'Blood! Blood!! Blood!!!' they shouted in chorus, cheering on the girls as if they were taking part in a harmless sports contest. Their calls fanned the flames of violence, and turned the girls into beasts. They attacked each other ever more brutally, inflicting deep wounds on one another, and when Patricia managed to throw Shannon to the ground, the crowd applauded as if a goal had just been scored in a football match. Shannon received a heavy kick in the middle of her face, and for a few seconds everything swam in front of her eyes. She thought her jaw had been dislocated. The pain was terrible. Then Patricia kicked her repeatedly in the ribs, winding her completely. Her whole body seemed to be one devastated mass, and the searing pain left her almost unconscious.

But she steeled her will and fought against the pain, and driven on by the merciless jeering of the audience she made one final effort, gathered herself together with a single blood-curdling cry, and before Patricia knew what was going on, Shannon had fallen on her, wedged her body between her legs, grabbed the knife with her two hands and stuck it repeatedly into her breast. Patricia tried desperately to defend herself, but it was no longer any use. A strange gurgling noise came from her throat as she fell limp under the shower of deadly stabs. The knife slipped from her hand, her eyes, distressingly dilated, glazed right over, and her head fell to one side. The game was over.

Shannon moved away from the dead body, shaking; she tried to stand up, stumbled, and collapsed next to the murdered girl. She heard the raging applause from the crowd and felt a hand on her shoulder. When she looked up, Paul was standing in front of her.

'Hey, Shannon. Welcome to the Jaguars.' He gave her a congratulatory pat on the back, and disappeared into the crowd.

'Hey, well done,' someone else praised her, and lots of kids, some of whom she knew and some of whom she didn't, congratulated her.

'You fought like a real Jaguar!'

'You're one of us, girl!'

'Keep it up! We can always use people like you!'

Shannon wasn't listening. The voices melted into one thick fog of noise. The figures swam before her eyes, turning into distorted shadows. She stared at her bloody hands and the bloody knife, and everything began to spin around her. She had killed someone. With her own hands. She had killed Patricia. She was a murderer. A murderer. The blood stuck to her hands. Patricia's blood. She had stabbed her to death. Pitilessly. She was guilty. Guilty of the death of a girl. A ten-year-old girl – ten years old, just like her. What had she done! Her hands shook, her whole body shook. She tried to get up, but tumbled forwards, her hands clutching her stomach; she hit the cold ground with her forehead, and had to throw up. She had nothing more than a bitter yellow liquid to retch. There was nothing more in her stomach. Then she collapsed on to her side.

8

The battle

All night long Shannon was haunted by horrific scenes from the murder she had committed. Patricia jumped on her, grabbed her by the neck, strangled her, and suddenly her face became horribly distorted and she broke out into hellish laughter. And when Shannon looked at her hands, they were covered in blood. She tried to wash away the blood, but she couldn't, and everything she touched started to bleed. And the blood gathered in one huge pool at her feet. Every so often, Shannon started out of her sleep; filled with a terrible panic and bathed in sweat she stared for a while into the darkness, her heart beating wildly, only to fall back into some other gruesome nightmare.

When she woke up the following morning, she found she was still lying on the same spot on the floor where she had collapsed the previous evening. A girl sat next to her. She must have been about the same age as her.

'Hi, I'm Peggy,' she said, and smiled. It was an enchanting smile. Shannon tried to get up, but even the smallest movement caused almost unbearable pain all over her body. She had been stabbed and brutally kicked dozens of times. Really, it was a miracle she was still alive.

'How late is it?' she asked in a weak voice, as she had lost all sense of time.

'Ten o'clock,' Peggy informed her. 'You screamed and moaned and blabbered weird stuff the whole night long.'

'Who says so?'

'I heard it myself.'

'You were here the whole night?'

'I thought that might be a good idea. I mean, Patricia had a good go at you.'

Shannon turned her head and established that Patricia had disappeared. Just for a moment she hoped it had perhaps all just been a bad dream and Patricia would suddenly turn up on the scene, laughing. But then Shannon saw the dried pool of blood that confirmed the terrible deed and brought her back to reality with a bump. She shivered. So it really had happened. She had done it. She had killed Patricia. It was awful.

'Where is she?'

'They took her away.'

'Where to?'

'I don't know.'

Shannon sat herself up with great effort and looked at her hands, on which the blood of her victim still stuck. She stared at these bloody hands, and wasn't far from howling, like a small child. But she didn't, even though she had never felt so lousy in her whole life before. She was disgusted by herself and by what she had done. The guilt of her crime bore down on her conscience like a huge rock, several tonnes in weight. She was the most miserable of all creatures. Cursed for eternity. She had killed a person. And everyone had enjoyed watching her do it.

Everyone.

Even Paul.

It was like a knife into her heart when she thought about that, and remembered how she had trusted him. She had thought he was her friend. She had thought she meant something to him. But she had been mistaken. He couldn't care less about her, he was completely indifferent to her. He had got a kick out of seeing her fear for her life, and if she had been the one killed in the fight to the death, he wouldn't have cried for her. It didn't really matter whether there was one more or one less. He had enough members in his big gang, enough girls who worshipped him. It was all just a game to satisfy his own ego and to prove his power. And she, Shannon, was nothing more than an unimportant little pawn within that game who could easily be dispensed with and whose loss wouldn't even really be noticed. This realisation pained Shannon more than the many injuries she had suffered so far.

'Why does he think up such things?' she suddenly asked Peggy. 'The whole thing was Paul's idea, wasn't it?'

'You mustn't take it too personally,' answered the girl. 'You're not the first person to be disappointed by him. Paul doesn't have any feelings. I've yet to meet someone who deals as cold-bloodedly as Paul. He's obsessed with himself, and calculating. Everything revolves around him. Always. To his advantage. And his reputation. He's a machine, not a person. In order to reach his goals he's prepared to trample over dead bodies if he has to, quite literally.'

'How was it with you?'

'I slept with him once. It was pure horror.'

'I didn't mean that. Did you also kill someone to . . . ?'

'Become a Jaguar?' The girl gave Shannon an understanding look. 'Was probably your first corpse, eh? You get used to it in time. It was just the same for me at first. But whoever's not prepared to kill doesn't belong in the Jaguars. You'll learn that for yourself.'

Shannon didn't know if that was what she wanted to learn. She found it repulsive. But she'd already done it once now. And that frightened her, really frightened her. The fact that Peggy spoke about it as if it were the most normal thing in the world shocked her even more. But she didn't let her uncertainty show. After all, she had left the fight victorious, and she would come to terms with her feelings of guilt herself. Somehow. It was just a matter of time. She tried to sit up a little straighter, but immediately howled out in pain.

'Perhaps we should disinfect the wounds first,' Peggy suggested knowledgeably.

'And what with?' asked Shannon.

Peggy held up a wine bottle triumphantly. 'This, for example.'

With the greatest of effort, Shannon managed to slip out of her trousers and t-shirt. Peggy helped her as she did so, and then set about washing off the dried blood with a wet rag, disinfecting the open wounds with wine and then bandaging them with torn strips of material. Shannon gritted her teeth bravely, and was relieved when Peggy had finished her work.

And then something strange happened. She laid her head on Peggy's lap to relax, and Peggy suddenly began softly stroking her face. Nothing like that had ever happened to her before. Nobody had ever stroked her face. Never. She had seen mothers with small children in films, and been amazed by how the women stroked and caressed their children. And she had always wished for such a mother herself, a mother who would take her in her arms and lovingly stroke her head, a mother who would fulfil her yearning for love and security. And when Peggy's delicate hands began to play with her hair, Shannon found herself wishing that she would never stop.

She looked up at Peggy. Their eyes met, and Shannon suddenly felt something strange happening inside her. She felt drawn to Peggy, as if by magic. Obviously Peggy felt the same, because suddenly she asked Shannon: 'How many times did you sleep with Paul?'

'Why do you want to know that?'

'Did you enjoy it?'

Shannon hesitated before replying. 'That's none of your business.'

'So you *didn't* enjoy it, am I right?'

'I said, that's none of your business.'

'It's strange,' Peggy continued, unabashed. 'In films it's always presented as if there were nothing nicer. The fact that there are women who are disgusted by the idea of going to bed with a man is a real taboo.'

Shannon gulped. Peggy had started on a topic that she didn't want to take any further, not under any circumstances.

'You know, after Paul had forced me to … you-know-what with him … that wasn't love. It was hell, I tell you. I'd had it up to here with boys. Absolutely. And then Jeanette appeared.'

'Jeanette?!'

'Yeah. She came across me when I was crying. I told her what had happened between me and Paul, and she began to comfort me. Well, I don't know who felt it first. But in any case I suddenly felt overcome by a whole pile of completely new feelings. First of all I fought against it, thought it wasn't normal, or whatever, but then I let it happen, and suddenly I realised that it wasn't half as bad as I'd originally thought.'

'Why are you telling me all this?' Shannon interrupted.

Peggy shrugged her shoulders. 'I thought you might be interested.'

'Well, I'm not,' countered Shannon dismissively. She didn't want to admit to either Peggy or herself that she very probably was. She didn't want to reveal the pile of completely new feelings, as Peggy had called them, that were starting to take hold of her. Peggy bent over her, and her long black hair tickled Shannon's face.

'Don't you think we'd make a good couple?' she whispered in her ear.

Shannon fought with her own feelings. 'Hey, did you have some sort of an idea that I might be a lesbian?'

'Don't be so hard on yourself. What's wrong with it? You feel it too, don't you?'

'I don't feel anything at all!' shouted Shannon. 'I'm not one of them! And now leave me alone!'

Peggy looked hurt. 'Whatever,' she said sulkily and pushed Shannon's head from her lap. 'If you prefer the president . . . Personally, I wouldn't do it to myself.' She got up and walked off jauntily. Shannon watched her go and already regretted having snarled at her so. She would apologise when she next got the chance. After all, Peggy had cleaned her wounds and otherwise been very kind to her. And then the way she had touched her and looked at her . . . She could have lost herself in Peggy's eyes. Was that normal? Shannon wondered. Doesn't matter, she thought. It wasn't exactly standard practice either that a girl should carry out her first murder at the age of ten. Or at all. Who decided what was right and wrong, what was normal and what was abnormal? God? God had never bothered with her. And he would definitely be even less interested in her after her repulsive deed. There was no doubt about that.

The wounds healed amazingly quickly, and after two weeks Shannon felt strong enough to take part in the Jaguars' activities. Even if she did feel betrayed and bitterly hurt by Paul, she thought it wise not to let it show, neither to him nor to the others. Feelings didn't belong in the Jaguars. And she *was* a

Jaguar, something she was proud of. She had the gang's symbol tattooed on to her right arm, and Paul taught her how to steal motorbikes and attack people. She enjoyed it, and was a quick learner.

One day Paul told her there was going to be a battle between them and Rage. Up until then, Shannon hadn't taken part in any of these infamous battles, but she was wildly keen finally to be allowed to go along.

'We're going to meet in the park behind the Catholic church. That's neutral ground.'

'What does neutral ground mean?'

'It doesn't belong to any gang. It's no-man's land. That means neither gang has to enter enemy territory to fight.'

'And what's the fight about?'

'New territories.'

'What's the point of that?'

'The same as in real wars. The more land you have, the more profit you can gain from it.'

'I don't understand.'

'It's very simple. The school, for example, where we met each other, is in Jaguars' territory. That means only *we* can sell drugs there, the Jaguars. No one else.'

'And people stick to that?'

'It's an unwritten law. Whoever sells drugs on another gang's land pays with his life.'

'So these gang wars are all about drugs?'

'They're about everything, but drug dealing in the first instance. That's why Big Q decides what areas we must fight for.'

'Big Q?'

'That's what we call the man whose drugs we sell. He's one of the most important people in Cleveland. He pulls all the strings. But no one knows who he is, no one except Johnny, the middleman, and Edmond, the war minister. And even they only get to see him when it's absolutely necessary; they don't know his real name, either. For all of us he's just simply the mysterious "Big Q".'

'So this Big Q is your boss, so to speak?'

'In a certain sense, yes. But as long as the sales figures are all right, he doesn't care about the rest. And in order to increase the profit, we continuously have to try to expand our territory. And that's only possible if we go to war with other gangs for it, because every part of town, every street, every square, belongs to some group or other.'

'And how do you know who's won a battle?'

'That's pretty easy. The winner is the gang who makes the other gang flee the field, or who leaves with more survivors.'

'Oh,' murmured Shannon, impressed by how matter-of-factly Paul could speak about these things.

'Yesterday Edmond and I met the president and war minister of Rage to fix the time, place and weapons. We agreed to permit everything this time, even firearms.'

'Isn't that always allowed?'

'That depends on what we've agreed,' Paul explained. 'One of the members of Rage brought along a revolver once, even though we had expressly said that we would only fight with knives. So of course there were lots more dead on our side as a result. It wasn't fair. And so we took revenge. Edmond and two others followed the boy, and watched until they were sure he was alone. Then four of us lay in wait for him and killed him, slowly and painfully.'

Shannon gulped. She still hadn't got used to how Paul could be so entirely unaffected when he told such macabre stories.

'It's your first battle, isn't it?'

'Yes.'

'One thing has to be clear to you right from the start: a Jaguar only leaves the field when *everybody* leaves the field. We fight side by side, as *one* man, whatever happens, even if you're more scared than you've ever been before. I don't tolerate any weaklings. I take personal care of anyone who leaves the field without my permission. You can count on that, as sure as I'm the president of the Jaguars.' Shannon didn't doubt it for a minute. Paul was capable of anything. Even that.

'Anything else?' she asked.

'Yes,' answered Paul, putting a revolver into Shannon's hands, 'I think you could use this.'

'Wow!' cried Shannon, looking at the revolver in her hands. 'That's for me?'

'A little present for you,' said Paul.

Shannon was absolutely delighted, even though the idea of aiming it at someone almost frightened the life out of her. 'Thanks, Paul!' she murmured, weighing the weapon in her hands. It was an indescribable feeling, a feeling of power, a feeling of being able to defend herself at any time from anything and anyone, to never again have to suffer bullies.

'I hope you know how to use it.'

'You can count on it.' She grabbed hold of the revolver with both hands, turned around quickly, narrowed her eyes slightly and aimed at a window pane, her arms outstretched.

'Bang!' she said, and automatically lifted her arms slightly. 'Not another step, or I'll shoot!' She felt like James Bond personified.

'Just remember that this evening you're not aiming at window panes,' said Paul drily, 'you're aiming at people.'

Shannon lowered her weapon. 'Don't you think I know that,' she replied, just as drily, and put the revolver casually into her jeans. She didn't let her fear show. A Jaguar didn't show any fear, ever. And as for how she felt inside, she'd come to terms with that herself at some stage.

It was a starry night. The Jaguars gathered behind the cemetery of the Catholic church at ten o'clock. The battle was set for eleven. They were all armed to the teeth: baseball bats, bike chains, metal pipes, knives, handmade maces, sawn-off shotguns, revolvers, pistols and other firearms. Most of them had psyched themselves up on heroin, cocaine and speed in order to overcome their fear. Shannon had shot some heroin, so the whole thing left her entirely indifferent.

The president gave a few instructions. Each sub-group should try to stay as close together as possible to provide cover for one another. Apart from that, they were planning to storm the park from the west, as soon as Paul gave the sign. Noiselessly the Jaguars lay in wait. Over two hundred pairs of eyes spied through the bushes into the murky park, where by day children laughed and flew kites, families picnicked and lovers sat on the pretty green benches. But now, a little before eleven o'clock at night, the park with its tall trees and majestic cathedral in the background seemed anything other than idyllic. It was ghostly. Only the sound of the wind whispering through the tops of the trees and the excited breathing of the kids behind them was to be heard. Otherwise nothing. The calm before the storm.

Shannon thought she could make out the shadows of figures behind some trees about a hundred metres away from them. She took hold of her revolver. Whatever was waiting for her out there in the darkness didn't frighten her – in fact she couldn't care less. She wouldn't shy away from shooting. She would fight like a real Jaguar.

'Well, Shannon, how are you feeling?' whispered Rick, who was lying right next to her in the grass, propped up on his elbows.

Shannon grinned. 'I'll kill them all, you'll see.'

'Just remember: you've only got five bullets.'

'Only five bullets?' said Shannon, surprised. 'You're not kidding, Rick?'

'So no crazy shooting around all over the place, okay?'

'No problem,' answered Shannon, and looked at her revolver. 'Five bullets. And I'll finish off the rest of them with this.' She showed Rick her flick-knife and then put it back in her trousers. At that moment a shot broke the silence, the sign for attack.

'Attack!!! Down with Rage!!!' Shouting wildly, the Jaguars stormed eastwards across the park, in the direction from which the Rage gang, with equally terrifying cries, were appearing from behind the bushes and the trees. The enemy gangs ran towards each other, slinging their weapons, and in the blink of an eye the park that was so peaceful by day had turned into one huge site of bloody slaughter. Shots were fired, screams echoed on the night air, all over the place youths were either falling to the ground or taking on one enemy after another with their murderous weapons. Some rolled heavily across the grass, locked in battle with an opponent, others chased each other with sharpened knives right through the centre of it all. It was a terrible bloodbath, and in the darkness it was difficult to tell the groups apart. The Jaguars could only be distinguished from their opponents by their black leather jackets.

Shannon was right in the middle of it all. She fired one shot indiscriminately into the crowd; she wasted another on a boy who was dragging himself away, and missed. Suddenly something whistled through the air. She turned around and saw herself faced with a huge guy who was preparing to attack her with a bicycle chain, but she just managed to get out of the way in time and the dangerous weapon swished inches past her head. Before her attacker could come a second time,

Shannon grabbed her revolver and fired two shots at him. The boy cried out, the chain slipped from his hands and Shannon snapped it up while her opponent fell in a heap on the ground. At the same time, she felt a searing pain. A boy had stabbed her from behind with his knife in her right shoulder. Raging, Shannon whipped the chain in his direction, hit him on the head, and thereby won time to take her own knife out of her trouser belt. She fell on the boy and stabbed him repeatedly, until he went limp.

Shannon stepped over his body, put her knife back in, and watched from behind as a strong Rage fighter armed with an iron bar knocked the knife out of the hand of one of the Jaguars. The Jaguar was facing his enemy unarmed, and knew that the iron bar was going to be the end of him. Unless a miracle happened. Shannon gripped her revolver, and just as the Rage lifted up the bar for the deadly blow, she shot him in the back. The boy fell forwards to the ground and lay lifeless next to his murderous weapon, and Shannon lifted her head to see whose life it was she had just saved.

And then both of them, Shannon and the boy in front of her, gaped at each other in amazement. The boy standing in the darkness before her and who she had just saved from certain death was none other than Robby!

'Robby!' Shannon cried out. She couldn't manage anything else. He didn't say a word, but the relief on his face was obvious. War was raging all around them, and they stood opposite one another, two lost children who had found each other again in what was probably the most unlikely of situations. They only looked at each other for a few seconds during the battle, but Shannon felt as if time was standing still. Everything around her fell silent, and they, he and she, were the only ones there. Robby and Shannon. The moment seemed to last for ever. It was the moment of a lifetime, unique and unforgettable, a moment that stirred up thousands of feelings in her, feelings like a cloud of colourful butterflies.

But then all of a sudden she felt a searing pain in her back, the park began to spin before her eyes, and she lost consciousness.

9

Robby

By the time she had come round again, it was light. She was lying in the factory hall on a blanket, her upper body so tightly wrapped in strips of cloth that she thought she was wearing a corset. At the least attempt to move she was overcome by a piercing pain in her back.

'Don't move!' warned someone. Shannon turned her head to the side and saw Rick sitting on the ground next to her.

'What happened?' she asked.

'Was probably a baseball bat or something,' explained Rick. 'You've probably broken a rib. And you got yourself a nice deep stab-wound as well. But it'll heal.'

'Did we win?'

Rick smiled. 'Yes. Rage fled.'

'Cool,' said Shannon. 'And who brought me back here?'

'I don't know. Paul said some long-haired guy carried you the whole way here.'

'Robby,' Shannon murmured straight away.

'Robby?' repeated Rick. 'Isn't that the way-out hippy guy?'

'You know him?'

'He's sold me a lot of motor-bikes, if *that's* the guy you mean. And as far as I know, he's great on the guitar.'

'You can certainly say that.'

'How do you know him?'

'From Los Angeles.'

'Los Angeles?'

'We were at the same party, and he wrote me a song. That was a year and a half ago. I thought I'd never see him again. And then yesterday night, all of a sudden there he is in front of me. In the middle of the battle. Just like that. I hadn't the faintest idea that he belongs to the Jaguars.'

'There are so many people in our gang. It's easy to lose sight of some.'

'I have to find him. Do you know where he is?'

'Cool it, Shannon. First of all you're going to lie here like a good girl, until that there has healed.'

'Will it take long?'

'A few weeks at the most.'

'I can't wait that long. I want to speak to him *now*.'

'The less you move, the quicker it'll be.'

'Couldn't you go and look for him for me?'

Rick grinned. 'Must be something like true love.'

'You don't understand.'

'Well, anyway, I reckon if he wants to speak to you, he'll turn up here of his own accord. And if he doesn't, then you'll know how things stand.'

He *didn't* turn up, not once in all those weeks. But that didn't discourage Shannon in the least. She was determined to find him, even if she had to look all over Cleveland for him. She pestered all the Jaguars with questions. Most of them couldn't help her at all, and the few who claimed to know him didn't know where he was at the moment. It was as if the ground had opened and swallowed him up. Nevertheless, Shannon didn't give up. Robby still belonged to the same gang as her. Somebody *had* to know where he was! But only after many disappointments did Shannon finally find the information she was seeking. Robby lived with a Miss Brown, whom he had accompanied on a mystic journey to Los Angeles. However, he had been back in Cleveland for the last two days.

Shannon made a note of the address and went straight there.

It was a block of flats, and Miss Brown's flat was on the sixth floor. Shannon rang the bell, and after a lengthy weight Robby appeared at the door. His long unkempt hair fell messily into his face. He was wearing a grass-green pair of trousers covered in bright spots, an orange shirt that screamed out to the heavens, and a black jacket. Around his neck hung a leather chain with a blue stone, and on his fingers he wore rings with mysterious symbols. He had a cigarette stuck in the corner of his mouth. He was quite taken aback by the unexpected visit.

'Hi,' said Shannon by way of a greeting. 'Can you tell me why you're spying on me?'

The boy ran his hands through his tangled hair and shook his head in amusement. 'First, let's get one thing straight: if anybody's spying on anyone here, then that's *you* on *me*. How did you find out my address?'

'Since when have you been a member of the Jaguars?'

'A little longer than you, that's for sure. What are you doing here?'

'The question is: what are *you* doing here?'

'I live here.'

'You don't need to tell me that.'

'So why do you ask?'

Shannon said nothing for a moment, confused. She would

have liked to ask Robby thousands of questions, but for some reason she couldn't manage anything now that she was standing in front of him. And then there was this strange feeling of being linked to him, like that time in Los Angeles, even though there was no logical explanation for it.

'I . . . I just wanted to thank you for carrying me back,' she eventually muttered, rather clumsily.

'Thanks for saving my life,' returned Robby. They looked at one another, and for a moment neither of them knew what to do next. Robby was the first to break the embarrassed silence.

'Do you want to come in? Miss Brown is at some sort of spiritual sitting, and she won't be back until this evening.'

He stepped to one side to allow Shannon to enter. The apartment was cramped and grubby. Abstract pictures and indefinable objects hung all over the place. Robby led the girl into his room, shifted a heap of dirty washing from the mattress to behind the wardrobe, and gestured to Shannon to sit down. There were posters of Bob Marley and some other music groups on the walls. Magazines, a packet of crisps, Robby's guitar and his shoes were thrown around on the floor. An incense stick glowed on a small, shabby table. It wasn't any cosier here than in the factory hall.

'Well,' said Robby, sitting with his legs crossed over each other on the floor, 'are you still as enthusiastic about your father as you were the last time we met?'

'I ran away.'

'That doesn't surprise me.' He took a drag from his cigarette, rested it on the ashtray and reached for his guitar. Then he strummed a few chords, looked fleetingly at the ceiling as if he were trying to remember something in particular, and suddenly began to sing a song.

'She came from Brazil to a foreign country, a little girl with big dreams. And the dreams kept her alive. Don't give up, little girl, don't give up, and don't lose sight of your dreams. Because you're lost without your dreams.'

Robby looked at her, and Shannon shivered. She remembered the song – remembered it well, in fact. But the fact that Robby, despite having made up the song for her on the spur of the moment over a year ago, could still remember the words and melody so precisely, really took her aback.

'You can remember it? Just like that?'

'I can sing you a second verse,' said Robby, and, fixing Shannon with his big, melancholy eyes, he carried on composing:

'And if the bitterness of life smothers your dreams, little girl, well, don't be discouraged. Somewhere there is someone who shares your dreams with you – just like the suffering, which you have learned to bear. Don't you ever forget that, little girl from Brazil, don't you ever forget that.'

Shannon didn't know what to say to that. Once more, she felt this inexplicable urge to open up to Robby, to trust him with things she had never told anyone else. But she didn't quite dare.

Robby played a few bizarre chords.

'I know what you've been through,' he said, 'better than you think. Your father promised you heaven on earth in order to tempt you to the USA. And he did everything in his power to keep your mother away from you.'

Shannon felt her pulse quickening. She looked at Robby in utter confusion. 'What do you know about my mother?'

He shrugged his shoulders. 'I know that she was a dancer.'

'How do you know that?'

'She got an offer to go and dance in Japan. Your father sent you to Brazil at the same time as your mother travelled to Japan. She never came back.'

Shannon gulped. This Robby was slowly beginning to give

her the creeps. 'How do you know all of this,' she asked uncertainly.

'My uncle told me.'

'And who's your uncle?'

'Federico. You know, the Satanist from Los Angeles. I lived with him for several years.'

'Federico is *your* uncle?'

'Yes, Shannon.'

'But . . . but then that would mean . . .'

Robby nodded. 'That's right.' He paused and looked intently at her. 'I'm your brother, Shannon.'

For a moment Shannon simply sat on the mattress with her mouth wide open, staring at Robby as if he were an alien. She felt as if her heart had stopped beating. She was incapable of formulating even one clear thought. What Robby had just told her was too much. That could never be true! That sort of thing just couldn't happen! It wasn't possible!

'I can imagine you weren't expecting that. But it's true, Shannon. We're brother and sister. I'm Robert, your brother, four years your senior.'

Shannon didn't know whether she should believe Robby or not. The whole thing was just too crazy to be true. But it would have been even crazier to make up something so incredible. Why? And if it were made up, then how did Robby know so much about her family? And what about this strange pull that she had felt right from the first moment when they met in Los Angeles?

'I know it sounds crazy. But it's the gospel truth,' Robby tried to convince her. 'What Dad did to you, he did all that to me as well. He often tortured me. He beat my head against the wall, held it down the toilet. I was too small to defend myself. I hadn't a hope. I presume you know what I'm talking about.'

She certainly did – all too well, in fact – and slowly she was beginning to believe his claims.

'When Dad sent you to Brazil and Mum went to Japan, I spent a while with Mum's mother and then went to Uncle Federico. I met Miss Brown at one of his mystic parties. She believed I was the reincarnation of her dead dog, and took me into her care. So I came to Cleveland. That was two years ago.'

Shannon still couldn't quite believe it. 'I've got a brother,' she murmured, shaking her head in disbelief. 'Why didn't you say anything, Robby?'

'It wouldn't have changed anything for you.'

'But I hadn't a clue! My dad . . . our dad . . . he never said anything about me having a brother.'

'Because I don't exist, as far as he's concerned. He never accepted me as his son. He tied me to the bed, punched me with his fists and told me I wasn't his son. I was born out of wedlock. I don't even have a birth certificate.' He took a drag from his cigarette and looked with narrowed eyes at the opposite wall. 'He mistreated Mum as well. He forced her to go to bed with him, he hit her. And as for me, I lay rolled up in a ball in the corner and had to watch it all happen. I was three years old when she got pregnant with you.'

Shannon gulped. His descriptions hit her hard and unexpectedly. It was almost too much for a ten-year-old girl. She felt as if someone had just stuck a knife right into the middle of her heart. It hurt like hell.

'What else do you know about her?' she asked in a quiet voice.

'She was very musical. I never saw her dance, but she had a fantastic voice. Sometimes she sang me to sleep.'

'Did she . . . did she like me?'

Robby hesitated before answering. Shannon felt herself getting hot.

'She was often away from home,' muttered Robby, and gave Shannon another one of his melancholy looks, 'but I'm sure she loved you very much.'

Shannon fought with her own feelings. She was all mixed up, hurt. She felt a lump in her throat, but she pulled herself together and swallowed it forcefully down.

'And why did she never come to visit me?'

Robby took Shannon's hand. 'Hey, little sister. Let's leave the past be. Today, only you and I count. And I reckon that's worth something.'

Shannon nodded. He was probably right. You couldn't turn back the hand of time to change certain things or to stop them from happening. So it was better to concentrate on the here and now. Only the two of them counted, and the fact that they had found one another.

'You know, I think a higher power was at work to bring us together,' said Robby. 'In any case, I wouldn't still be alive if it weren't for you.'

'What a strange coincidence,' considered Shannon. 'Without knowing it, I saved my own brother's life.'

'For which I will be eternally grateful, little sister,' said Robby, and pressed her hand.

She smiled. 'You're welcome, big brother.'

They sat across from one another in silence for a while, and the silence seemed almost ceremonial.

She had a brother – that was all Shannon could think of, and the longer she thought about it, the happier and prouder she became. It was the best present she had ever had. A brother.

And his name was Robby.

10

The pact

Robby and Shannon soon became inseparable. Not a day went by when they didn't take drugs together. They did everything together. When they stole motorbikes or cars, they felt they were masters of the universe. Everything belonged to them – the street, the cars, the houses, the people, the whole world – and so they were only taking what was rightfully theirs. Robby also taught Shannon how to hold up small shops, and in the battles between the gangs the pair nearly always fought side by side, brother and sister, prepared to defend each other to the very end.

Their friendship was so unusual that Paul argued with Shannon on many occasions and accused her of loving her brother more than she loved him. Her relationship to Paul really wasn't the same as before; it hadn't been for a long time – to be more precise, not since that cursed day when she had committed her first murder. Paul had stood by and watched the worst minutes of her life without even batting an eyelid – Paul, who had always been so understanding in the school yard. She had never forgiven him for that, and it hung over them like a dark cloud. Her close relationship to Robby deepened the split between her and Paul even further, but she didn't care. She didn't need anyone else to protect her or introduce her to the world of drugs and crime. She had learned enough to be able to lead her life as *she* saw fit. She didn't let anyone tell her what to do and what not to do, not even the president himself. And if she preferred to spend her time with Robby rather than with Paul, then she was perfectly entitled to do so.

'You fed me to the lions that time,' she accused Paul, when he brought up the subject again, 'so don't play the violins now. You lost me months ago. And on top of that, Robby is my brother, not my lover.'

'Still a bad swap,' said Paul, 'a president for a meaningless junkie. Lots of girls would die to spend just one night with me.'

'Then you can count me out of your harem.'

'You're forgetting that I'm the president. Every Jaguar girl is available for me, if I want her. That's an unwritten law. You can't change that.' He grabbed her by the arm and pulled her to him. But she tore herself away.

'Find yourself another girl. You've got a big enough selection.'

'I like wild girls,' he answered and tried to grab her for a second time. But she got away. No, she didn't want to have anything more to do with Paul, that was definite. He thought he could do whatever he fancied, just because he was the president of the Jaguars. He didn't have a heart, or if he did then it was one of stone.

Robby was quite different in that respect. He hated violence. He took part in the street fights all right, attacked people and sold drugs, but in his heart he was one of the most peaceful people Shannon had ever known.

For her eleventh birthday she travelled with Robby to Lake Erie. It was a bitingly cold winter day. An icy wind blew over the huge lake and even penetrated through the thick coats they had stolen from a clothes shop. Shannon loved this lake; it was so big that you couldn't see to the other side. She loved the endless water, and she envied the birds that circled tirelessly over the limitless expanse without meeting even the least resistance. These birds were unburdened and carefree, as unburdened and carefree as Shannon sometimes longed to be herself.

In spite of the biting cold she sat with Robby on a bench under a large tree, and Robby ceremoniously presented his little sister with a birthday present. It was a necklace made out of leather with a blue stone attached to it. The stone was flat, polished and had a big hole in the middle of it.

'Wow,' said Shannon, putting the leather chain around her neck, 'it's beautiful. Thank you.'

'It used to belong to me,' explained Robby, 'the pattern and colour of the stone are a symbol for my soul. When you wear the stone, I'm always nearby.'

'Cool,' said Shannon, even though she thought the whole thing with the soul was a bit weird. But she knew her brother and his strange ideas about the 'ancient powers of the universe'.

'I wear almost the same chain, but with a green stone,' continued Robby, pulling out his chain from underneath his coat, 'that's supposed to be a symbol for *your* soul. When we both wear these stones and think of one another, we'll be united for ever.'

'Do you really think so?' ventured Shannon, doubtfully.

'I read it somewhere,' said Robby. 'But there's definitely something to it, believe me. Our life on this earth is a journey, and when we reach our destination, we become immortal.'

'Do you really believe in that?'

'Of course. And love will unite everything, most of all those who have loved one another on this earth. Wherever we are, whether in this world or the next: when we think of one another, our souls will find each other and we will be together for eternity.'

'Sounds good,' said Shannon, and looked at the blue stone around her neck. 'Together for eternity.' Even though she only rarely managed to follow Robby's logic, there was nevertheless something fascinating in his philosophy. Perhaps it simply came from Robby and his way of speaking. Sometimes Shannon felt he was wearing an invisible pair of glasses that allowed him to perceive his environment quite differently from everybody else. He had his own interpretation of terms such as fate, God, death and eternity, and Shannon very much enjoyed diving into her brother's alternative world. She could spend hours listening to his explanations and watching his transfigured face as he spoke. When she lost herself in his thoughts she managed, at least for a short while, to break out of her own grey world and to dream of a more colourful, happy one. Her brother clung on to these images as if they were a lifebuoy, and she herself clung on to his belief. As long as he gained strength from it, she would also believe in this strength. Some of it at least had to be true. After all, her brother couldn't be completely wrong.

The other Jaguars tended to laugh at him for his unusual views.

'You're brother's all right,' Rick once said to Shannon, 'but he doesn't have much of a clue about supernatural powers. If you want, I'll take you to a meeting this evening, where messages really do get through.'

'What kind of a meeting?'

Rick winked at her. 'A Satanic one,' he said in a low, mysterious voice.

Shannon had nothing against it, and went along. They travelled for over an hour on their motorbikes until they reached the black building where the meeting was to be held which, according to Rick, was supposed to be so great.

When they entered, the Satanic worship had already begun. The murky circular room, reminiscent of a circus tent, held about eighty people. The audience came from all different social spheres, from business people in ties to reeking drug-addicts. The walls were painted with crescents and five-pointed stars. Black, violet and red curtains hung everywhere, bizarre guitar sounds mixed with the smell of burning flesh and incense. It was a terrifying atmosphere. It was as if all the powers of darkness really had gathered here in this one room, as if they floated invisibly under the roof, staring down with distorted grimaces on those present below.

Shannon felt lousy. She shivered and felt as if someone had robbed her of her vitality when she entered the room. They sat in the back row and along with the other people stared trance-like down into the arena, always with the frightening feeling that someone was watching them the whole time. Down in the middle of the arena was a long table on which various knives lay, and next to it was a type of oven, in which a live animal was being roasted over an open fire. Its squeals went right through Shannon. Doubtless she had found her way into the forecourt of hell itself, and she would have preferred to leave immediately, but her legs seemed to be made of lead.

A priest in red robes with a black gown appeared in the arena, raised his hands and called out into the crowd:

'We believe in Satan and his eternal kingdom, hell! There is no heaven. We will end up in hell, and so we call out to you all to be the devil's friends, even here on earth! Jesus came to this earth to destroy Satan's kingdom, but he was not successful.

And as long as the prince of darkness has enough worshippers, his greatest enemy Jesus is helpless against him!'

Shannon started. There it was again, that name: Jesus. That name that had driven her to beat up Nicolas that time, ages ago, when she had still gone to school. Jesus loves her, Nicolas had said. Shannon didn't want to hear anything of the sort. No one could love someone like her, and certainly not God.

'If I believe in anything, then in the devil. And that's why we wear his sign,' Paul had said. Shannon hadn't taken the whole thing with the number 666 too seriously, and had never thought about the devil. But on this evening she realised for the first time that he really did exist. And obviously Jesus was the bitterest enemy he had to fight. At least that was what the priest claimed, and his words wove their way through the listeners like dark scarves of mist, nailing them to their seats. His voice got louder and more intense. He began to speak in a strange language, forming words she had never heard in her life before.

And then it happened. He looked at her. Right at her. From out of the eighty people he chose her and looked up at her, and in spite of the poor light she could see his eyes. Crystal clear. A shiver went down her spine. Those were no human eyes that met hers, they were the most repulsive eyes she had ever seen, they were the eyes of an evil force that belonged in some terrible pit, they were the eyes of the devil himself. And then she heard his voice. Right next to her ear. He was whispering her name. He was telling her to come forward. She looked into the fiery red eyes of the priest, and possessed by some invisible force, she got up from her seat.

'The master has chosen you,' the priest pronounced in a hollow voice, 'in order to make a pact with you. He will grant you everything for which you wish.' He reached out his hands to Shannon, and she made her way over to him as if she were answering to some magnetic force. She knew what she would ask the master for. She had been tortured with nightmares since that terrible night, a year ago now, when she had killed a girl the same age as herself; night after night she had been tortured. How often had she woken up bathed in sweat and thought blood was dripping from her hands? Then she had hardly fallen asleep again before Patricia was chasing her with a knife, ready to kill her. They were terrible images, and they filled Shannon with a hellish fear. She would have given anything to conquer this fear. She was even prepared to enter into a pact with the devil if he granted her the peace she had so far failed to find herself.

The animal over the fire stopped squealing, but the total silence was almost worse. Shannon saw herself moving forwards, step by step, unable to stop herself. She no longer had any control over her body. She felt she wasn't herself any more. It was as if she were watching somebody else move to the front. She wasn't involved, even though she knew what she was doing. It was as if she were dead, but her feet moved towards the priest, entirely of their own accord, as if steered by some kind of unknown force.

A door opened. A second priest appeared, and in his arms he carried a live billy goat. Shannon had reached the centre of the ring, and stood in front of the two priests like a sleepwalker. She heard the second priest beginning to curse Jesus and worship the devil, and the crowd automatically joined in with his euphoric jubilations.

'The master has told me he will fulfil your wish,' said the other priest in a low voice, 'it will remain a secret between you and him. But in return you must make him a sacrifice on the first day of every month. And you will seal the pact with this victim.' He took a knife from the long table and passed it to Shannon. The second priest laid the billy goat on an altar, and before Shannon knew what she was doing, she had lifted the knife and stabbed out blindly. She didn't feel anything as she did so, nothing at all, no hatred or revenge, no pity or remorse, no fear and no sorrow. Nor did she feel a thing as she handed the knife back to the priest and the dead billy goat was carried away.

The crowd roared, clapped, rose out of their seats and screamed as Shannon turned around and staggered back to her seat like a remote-controlled robot. She had a pulsing headache. The whole room seemed to be applauding her, even the invisible ghosts whose eyes Shannon could feel on the back of her neck.

It was over.

She had paid the price.

She had given up her last spark of humanity in order to conquer her fear. With this sacrifice she had sealed a pact with Satan, and hadn't been in the least bit moved by it. She was no longer human: instead, she was a wild animal, devoid of a conscience. She no longer had a heart, or if she did then one of stone. She had become immune. Untouchable.

She had become like Paul.

And the devil was laughing down at her in contempt.

11

Big Q

'We'd like to speak to the doctor.'

'Do you have an appointment?'

'It's an emergency.'

'You can't see him without an appointment.' The heavily made-up young woman at the reception desk smiled regretfully at the youths. 'I'm sorry.' As far as she was concerned that was the end of the conversation, and so she returned to her paperwork.

It was a rainy cold Monday afternoon in February 1985. There were five of them there. Rick and Bob entered the doctor's surgery first, closely followed by Robby and Peggy; Shannon was between them, leaning heavily on both so as not to fall over. The anaesthetising effect of the heroin – which the thirteen-year-old had shot four hours earlier in order to get the spectacular fight over with as fearlessly and painlessly as possible – was already wearing off, and the pain from her numerous injuries was almost robbing her of her consciousness. Nobody had thought she would come out of it alive. Her opponent had been rated too dangerous. And she herself had been afraid – not of death, and not of killing someone, but of looking a coward.

When the young woman behind the counter realised that she hadn't managed to shake off the youths, she pursed her little red mouth and squeaked in a high voice: 'Like I said. Dr Johnson won't see anyone without an appointment. Try the hospital.'

'This is an emergency!' repeated Robby, pointing to his sister who hung groaning between him and Peggy. Repulsed, the woman took in the girl with the bright green hair. She looked as though she had been attacked by wolves. Her clothes were in rags and smeared with blood, and her left hand was wrapped in an equally blood-soaked cloth; the blood looked fresh.

'You need an appointment first. I'm sorry,' she said, repeating her one little line, but at that very moment she found herself looking down the barrels of four revolvers.

'We'd like to speak to the doctor!' snarled Rick, in no uncertain terms. The woman gasped for air like a fish out of water, incapable of saying a single word.

'And *without an appointment!*' emphasised Robby.

'Yes . . . of course,' she stammered and reached with her index finger for the intercom. 'Doctor . . . there are . . . there are some young people here, who . . ..' She didn't get any further. Bob leaned over the counter and grabbed her by the arm.

'Take us to him, lady!'

'Of . . . Of course,' she said, pale as a ghost in spite of her heavy make-up. Bob pushed her in front of him like a shield, down a narrow corridor and into the consultation room. The others followed him, their weapons drawn.

The doctor, a friendly looking older man in a white coat, looked up from his desk in shock. Bob held his gun to the hostage's temple, causing her to cry out shrilly.

'Shut your mouth!' shouted Bob, and turned to the doctor. 'One false move, doc, and your colleague here is dead!' The man in the white coat didn't move an inch. Only his eyes moved, quickly taking in the dangerous customers and automatically resting on the girl with the grass-green hair. The atmosphere was tense. The air in the white room seemed to buzz with the tension.

'We need your help,' Robby explained. 'She's lost a lot of blood.'

The doctor looked the girl up and down. 'What happened?' he wanted to know.

Robby hesitated before replying.

'She was attacked,' Rick explained.

'When?'

'About an hour ago.'

'And who are you?'

'Friends,' said Robby vaguely. Given the circumstances, the doctor had to be content with the vague answers; he nodded towards a stretcher.

'Lay her down there,' he ordered, and his voice sounded surprisingly calm, given the unusual situation. 'I'll do what I can.'

'We'd certainly suggest you do,' said Bob, and when the man remained sitting, he shouted at him nervously: 'What are you waiting for? Do something!'

The doctor raised his hands slowly. 'It's hard to work with three weapons pointing at me.'

'A lame excuse,' growled Bob. 'A doctor who can't work under pressure is good for nothing.'

'I'd rather he does a good job than botch it because of our weapons,' said Robby. 'We've got a hostage after all, in case he tries anything stupid.'

'Okay,' agreed Rick, nodding to Peggy and Robby. 'But no funny business, doc. If you try to pull a fast one, your lady will pay the price.'

They hid their weapons away under their t-shirts. Only Bob kept his revolver pointing at the young receptionist, who was shaking like a leaf and thought her last hour had come.

Shannon lay on the stretcher, her face contorted in pain, and pressed Peggy's hand.

'Hey, Shannon, hang on in there,' said Peggy encouragingly, and Robby added: 'I'm right here beside you, little sis.'

Dr Johnson got up and walked measuredly over to the patient. His small eyes looked calm and trustworthy as he bent down over Shannon and asked her her name. He considered her contracted pupils, and pushed up the sleeves of her jumper to confirm his suspicion. 'You've shot heroin, Shannon, haven't you?'

'We fought,' murmured Shannon.

'Who?'

'The Apache and me.'

'Who's the Apache?'

'Hey, doc!' growled Rick, pushing himself threateningly between Robby and Peggy. 'You're a doctor, not a reporter.'

Dr Johnson examined Shannon quickly from head to toe, and the girl moaned at even the slightest touch. Her whole body seemed to be one single open wound. The doctor shook his head repeatedly. 'My God, that doesn't look good.'

'Have a look at her hand, doc!' said Peggy in concern. 'She bled the whole way here, like a pig. Have a look at it!' The scrap of material she had wrapped around Shannon's left hand really was soaked through with blood. Carefully, the doctor took hold of Shannon's wrist and unwrapped the bloody cloth, Shannon groaning with pain. The wound was not a pretty sight. A knife had clearly been stabbed right through the palm of her hand.

'Can you move your fingers?'

Shannon tried to, with great effort.

'Not the thumb,' she said, gritting her teeth. 'It really hurts, doc!'

'I'll give you an injection against the pain,' decided the doctor. 'I hope it didn't hit a nerve. You'll need stitches in that as soon as possible. How did it happen?'

'I wanted to hold him by the arm,' Shannon explained quietly, as the doctor prepared the injection. 'But I got his knife. He speared me with it.'

She had the scene clearly before her eyes, saw the onlookers firing her on, saw Johnny, the muscular Apache, keeping his eyes fixed on her as he circled around her like a gladiator settling in for the kill, the chain in one hand, his knife in the other. And she stood across from him, a slim, thirteen-year-old girl, armed with a baseball bat, a knife and the unyielding will to win. Nobody had rated her chances very highly. Nobody had ever beaten the Apache: he had already successfully managed to defend his position as contact man for the drugs trade on several occasions, and he would do it again now. You could only take over somebody else's job if you killed them first. In order to rise up the ranks of the Jaguars, you literally had to do it over dead bodies, and Shannon was wildly determined to crack Johnny's monopoly in the drugs trade – a dangerous decision, as her own body had discovered.

It was probably the hardest duel of her life. The Apache threw the chain like a lasso towards her; the noose wound itself around her foot and brought her to the ground. Johnny rushed towards her with outstretched knife, and when Shannon tried to grab on to him by the arm, the Apache intercepted her and Shannon's hand found not his arm, but rather his knife, so that her hand was cut right through. A hellish pain seared through her, but Shannon knew that she mustn't give up. The two deadly enemies wrestled on the ground, got back to their feet, hit and stabbed each other with bats, chains and knives, rolled again on the ground and picked themselves up once more. Johnny's knife made shreds of Shannon's pullover and grazed just past her throat. Then he dealt her a hefty blow on the shin and she heard the sound of splintering bone. She let out a piercing scream, grabbed her knife and stabbed right through his calf in blind fury. Once again they rolled on the floor until this time she managed to jump on to his stomach and stick her knife into his chest.

On the way to the doctor's she had fallen unconscious several times and now, as she lay on the stretcher and the doctor examined her hand, she passed out once more. When she came round again, Dr Johnson was already in the process of cutting the leg of her trousers open in order to have a look at the broken shin bone. He was almost lost for words when he discovered all the stab wounds.

'Good grief! Just what on earth happened to this girl?'

'Do your work, doc,' said Rick coldly.

The doctor shook his head. 'Wouldn't you rather tell me the truth? Your friend is punctured all over with stab wounds!'

'Guess why we're here!'

'Then tell me what happened!'

'It was just a fight. And she won.'

'She won?! With a broken leg? One hand stabbed right through? Bruises, blood clots and stab wounds all over her body? Pumped full of heroin? If this girl won, what does the loser look like?'

'He's dead,' spoke up Shannon. 'I beat the Apache. Nobody thought I'd manage it. But I finished him off. And now his position belongs to *me*.'

The doctor looked at them all in dismay, hoping for an explanation. But none came. Instead, Rick said flatly, 'Just patch her back together again, doc. The rest is none of your business.'

And Bob added, in no uncertain terms: 'Just remember your lady here!'

The doctor looked from his secretary to the four teenagers and back to Shannon, and shook his head vehemently. 'You don't understand. I can't simply patch your friend back together again. This girl has to be taken to hospital straight away!'

'That's out of the question!'

'But what if she has internal injuries?'

'Shannon is tough,' Robby assured him, 'she's already survived other stuff.'

'I wouldn't bet on it this time.'

'You talk too much, doc.'

'I'm going to call an ambulance.'

At that moment, three revolvers were whipped out, and Rick walked slowly towards the doctor. 'You'll do no such thing, is that clear?'

The doctor gulped. The air was slowly beginning to get unbearably heavy. 'The hospital is equipped for this kind of an emergency,' he said, daring a second attempt.

But the kids wouldn't buy this either. Rick walked right up close to him and held his revolver under his nose. 'Listen up, man. We're the Jaguars. You'll find most of our leaders on the wanted list in any police station. Most of us have committed so many crimes that it's not worth counting any more. What, do you think, will happen if a girl like Shannon turns up at the hospital? Just think for a moment, doc! And have a little guess at what they'll do to Shannon if they get their hands on her! They'll lock her up in the young offenders' unit. Why do you think we didn't go to the hospital ourselves? We might just as well go straight to the cops. Get it now?'

'This girl's life is at risk!'

'*Your* life is at risk, Dr Johnson!' snarled Rick. 'If Shannon has to be operated on, then you're going to do that *here*! That's the last thing I'm going to say to you, so now you'd better come up with something pretty quick!'

Shannon heard the hectic conversation as if she were listening through cotton wool. She stared up at the harsh neon tube above her head and felt as if the lamp were beginning to spin. The light seemed to get weaker and weaker. Her brother's voice merged into the voices of all the others and seemed to fade further and further away, the scene began to swim before her eyes, and then everything went black.

When she came to again, Shannon didn't know what had happened. It took her a couple of seconds to realise she was lying in Robby's room. Her left leg was in plaster, her left hand heftily bandaged, and on various parts of her body she could feel large plasters and bandages. She almost felt like an Egyptian mummy. But, unlike a mummy, she was alive, and even the tiniest of movements caused her the most terrible pain.

'Hello, little sis!'

Shannon turned her head carefully, and saw Robby sitting next to her on the floor, guitar in hand.

'How're things?'

'I'll survive.'

Her brother smiled with relief. 'I said you were tough.'

'Was I out long?'

'A few hours. The doctor patched you up nicely. He stitched your hand and said it was almost a miracle that the knife didn't cut through a nerve. He also said that if we have another emergency, we shouldn't hesitate to call on him, no appointment necessary. He's a good guy really.'

'Did you think I'd manage it?'

'Of course I did.'

'I mean beating Johnny.'

Robby considered for a while. Then he looked deep into Shannon's eyes. 'I was worried about you,' he finally admitted. 'I was afraid of losing you, little sis.'

'I don't throw the towel in quite that easily, big brother.'

'I still worry about you, Shannon. What if something happened to either of us?'

'What's going to happen to us?'

'You have to promise me not to cry if I die.'

Shannon looked at her brother in dismay. 'What's all this about? You're not going to die.'

'Promise me. Promise me not to cry if I die.'

'Robby! We'll always be together. That's never going to change. Stop talking like that!'

'Promise me!' He laid his hand on her shoulder. His eyes were shining strangely. There was both despair and genuine concern in the look he gave her. Shannon had never seen her brother like this. It seemed as if his soul was desperately clinging to the one creature who had ever loved him.

'Promise me!' It was a cry from the very depths of his heart.

Shannon nodded. 'I promise you, Robby.'

Apart from Robby there was only one other person with whom Shannon had a particularly special relationship: Peggy. Shannon had liked her from the first moment she set eyes on her, but hadn't wanted to admit her feelings back then. But the sense of attraction had grown – every time she was together with Peggy, whenever Peggy brushed as if by accident against her or followed the lines of her body with her big green eyes. Eventually she didn't want to keep fighting it. She let herself be carried along by the torrent of completely new feelings, a stream which had its source in her own yearning for safety. She let herself be washed into the sea of love and bob there like a sailing ship without a captain, blown by the wind and the waves of her own passion.

It was a constant ebb and flow of seduction and surrender, of domination and submission, of encouragement and dismissal, and Shannon soon learned how to play this manipulative game. She learned how to make herself indispensable to another girl. She learned how to tie Peggy to her by giving her what she wanted — her own body — and took in return what she herself so desperately sought — a little human warmth.

For the first time in her life Shannon had the feeling that there was someone who could fill the emptiness her heart had felt for all those years. And so she needed Peggy. She needed her closeness, she needed her gentle touch, she needed Peggy just as she needed air to breathe. She was addicted to her. She was just as unable to survive without Peggy as she was without drugs. She needed to be loved by a woman; it filled a need in her which she herself couldn't articulate.

Perhaps it was because up until then she had only ever been disappointed and humiliated by men. Grandfather, Dad, Uncle Federico, Paul: they had all used her for their own purposes. None of them had ever done her a kind deed, not one of them. No, she had had it up to here with men — and Paul in particular, who thought she was just a sex object, incapable of thinking for herself, must finally realise now that not only machos could command respect. She was tougher than many of the boys, she had proved that yet again with her victory over Johnny. She had broken into the male domain. She had achieved what no Jaguar girl had managed before her: she was the first female go-between for the drug trade. And she was proud of it.

Shannon already knew how the drug trade worked. Her brother had taught her the most important rules of the game, and she had occasionally bought drugs or done smaller deals for one drug trader or another. But all of that was nothing compared to her business now. It was no longer a question of small quantities, a few grams here and there. Now she was looking at bigger quantities and sums of money that would make you dizzy. Now she was looking at business with Big Q.

On the Sunday morning in July when Shannon answered a call on the telephone in front of the factory, she immediately realised that something was up.

'Big Q wants to see you,' said an unfamiliar voice on the other end of the line, 'you and a certain Bob. He's expecting you in exactly one hour's time at Blue Eyes.'

'Why Bob?' Shannon asked. But the unknown caller had already hung up. Shannon didn't know what this meant. It wasn't the unfamiliar voice that unsettled her. Big Q always got a third person to pass on his messages. But why Bob? There were only two Jaguars who were allowed to meet Big Q face to face, and that was Edmond, the war minister, and Shannon, the contact woman for the drug trade. For all the others he was simply the mysterious Big Q, without name, address or face. Not even Paul, president of the Jaguars, had ever seen him. So why Bob?

Bob was unimportant. He was a member of a gang of twenty, the leadership of which Shannon had recently taken over. Their speciality was the drugs trade. Bob was a heroin addict, and Shannon liked him because he was a man of few words and acted instinctively in critical situations. She often used him in bigger drug deals so that he could cover her back in case of a set-up. Bob was eighteen years old, and internally as well as externally pretty shot from his heavy drug habit. So why Bob?

When Shannon told him that Big Q wanted to see him, he started.

'Big Q wants to see me? Why?'

'That's what I'd like to know. You haven't been up to anything, have you?'

'Of course not.'

'Strange,' muttered Shannon. 'Apart from Edmond and me, he's never called up anyone else. But we'll find out what it's all about.'

'Perhaps a secret mission?'

'No idea. Hopefully nothing bad.'

An hour later Shannon and Bob were at the agreed meeting place, Blue Eyes, a normal junction in the centre of Cleveland, where a white Mercedes pulled up, punctual to the minute. The rear door opened, a man dressed in black got out, pushed the two kids wordlessly into the back seat, and the car pulled away again, almost without a sound. Not a word was spoken. The driver concentrated on the road ahead, and Shannon and Bob sat squashed between two huge muscular men who spent the whole journey looking stubbornly ahead with faces as unfriendly as thugs in an American gangster film.

The journey lasted over forty minutes. They turned off the asphalt roads, travelling the last twenty kilometres through meadows and woods until they reached an imposing, beautifully decorated iron gate at the bottom of a green hill. An armed guard came towards them, glanced inside the vehicle, nodded, and the gate opened as if by magic. The little road snaked further along the hill, past a small lake, stables and wide, green fields. It was a dream landscape, and right in the middle of this untouched paradise there suddenly appeared an incredible villa, the sight of which made Bob's chin hit the floor.

'It's just his country home,' Shannon whispered. 'He lives somewhere in the city.'

They stopped in front of the palatial entrance with marble pillars and fountain. The two black-clothed heavies searched the kids for weapons before accompanying them along a corridor to a room whose front wall consisted of one single window with a breathtaking view of the hills. In the middle of the room there was a long, dark red mahogany table, set for two. Shannon was puzzled. Big Q had often had lunch with her and Edmond at this table and done business. Why had he only set the table for two this time?

The men left the room, and Shannon and Bob waited alone. They waited for over a quarter of an hour. Then a door opened, and Big Q came in. If you met him on the street, you wouldn't give him a second glance. He was a man of average height, about fifty, with a moustache and greying hair. He wore a white suit and tie and a pair of dark shades. His face was stiff and cold; it was the iciest face Shannon had ever seen, the face of a mafia baron, the face of someone it would be better not to annoy.

'Sit down,' was his only greeting, and he pointed to two leather chairs. His voice was rough and flat. He lit up a cigarette.

'So you're Bob,' he surmised, taking a deep drag from his cigarette and blowing the smoke up diagonally into the air. 'I'm sure you're wondering why I've asked you to come here.' He walked right up close to him, so close that Bob could feel the heat of his breath. 'I've heard of you, Bob. And I haven't particularly liked what I've heard.' Bob automatically sank a little lower into the chair; Shannon cast him a questioning look, but he avoided her eyes.

Big Q strolled comfortably across the room.

'How many kilograms of heroin was Zeppelin supposed to get?'

'Five,' said Shannon.

'Five,' repeated Big Q. 'And how many kilograms did I give you?'

'Five,' answered Shannon, 'plus 750 grams after we gave you the money.'

'Correct,' said Big Q. 'Just like any other deal: 750 grams for the Jaguars, 15 per cent.' He turned around and looked from one to the other.

'But Zeppelin rang me yesterday from New York, and said fifteen grams were missing. How can you explain that?'

Shannon's mouth dropped open. 'Fifteen grams?! But that's not possible!'

'Well, that's the case,' said Big Q, unmoved. 'Fifteen grams of heroin is a lot. Too much to have simply mislaid. And don't forget: Zeppelin came expressly from New York and paid cash for it, $22 per gram. He's pretty angry, as you can imagine. And he said I'd better sort it out.'

Shannon didn't know what to say or think any more. She peered over at Bob, who was sitting in silence with bowed head, chewing on his bottom lip. She didn't want to finish the thought that was suggesting itself to her. She called the scene back to mind.

The hand-over had taken place two days ago, on Friday evening at 11 p.m. The meeting place had been an empty building at the end of a disused road. Zeppelin had agreed that with Shannon over the phone. Zeppelin was a well-regarded drug dealer from New York and a long-standing customer of Big Q. Shannon had frequently brought him larger deliveries, and up until now everything had always gone well. They had stored the five kilograms of heroin in a sports bag, neatly packed into little plastic bags. Then they had hidden behind a container and waited for the customer. Everything went according to plan. Bang on 11 p.m. a car pulled up, turned off its lights and somebody could be heard getting out. A dark figure approached the container, briefcase in hand. Nothing was said. Shannon passed the bag with the drugs to the man, and he gave her the briefcase with the money; no words were exchanged, and no check was made. The man didn't look in the bag, Shannon didn't look in the briefcase. Both of them knew that neither of them would dare cheat on the other. The risk was too great. But obviously it had happened nevertheless. Fifteen grams were missing! Shannon hadn't taken any of it – why would she? The Jaguars' share of the profit was 15 per cent of each successful transaction, and of course she made sure to get her own share of that. So it must have been Bob. They were the only two present at the hand-over, there had been no one else. At some point when she wasn't paying attention he must have taken the fifteen grams, and she hadn't even noticed. That meant trouble, big trouble. They hadn't just pulled a fast one on some small drug dealer, but on Big Q himself. And Big Q was not to be messed with.

'Well, Bob, tell uncle your story,' said the mafia man, pacing his way comfortably around Bob's chair. 'Why did you do it? Why did you steal the fifteen grams? Did you think I wouldn't come after it?'

Bob gulped. 'I . . . I . . . I don't know anything.'

'No? And where are the fifteen grams?'

'I don't know.'

'Do you think Zeppelin would cheat on me? Or do you think I'd cheat on *him*?'

Bob shook his head.

'So how do you explain the missing heroin?' Big Q went up to the eighteen-year-old, took a deep drag from his cigarette and blew the smoke right into his face. 'That really wasn't very smart, Bob. It had to be one of you. And who do you think is the prime suspect?'

Bob chewed his bottom lip nervously as Big Q moved in even more closely on him. 'I've been having a little listen around. You're a heroin addict, aren't you? You can't last a day without the stuff. You'd do anything to get your drugs, wouldn't you?'

Bob didn't contradict him. His movements became increasingly uncontrolled; he didn't dare lift his eyes from the floor.

'Why did you do it?' the man whispered in his ear. 'Why, Bob? Why did you take the fifteen grams? Don't you know how much that costs? That's $330, my boy. You cheated Zeppelin out of $330, and me too.'

'I . . . I'll pay it back,' murmured Bob.

'So you admit taking it.' Big Q smiled. Bob sank even lower into his chair. He was a pitiful sight.

'I . . . I couldn't resist it. It was so much. So much . . . I didn't think anyone would notice a few grams.'

'Is that what you thought?'

'It won't happen again, I promise.'

'No, it certainly won't. Whoever cheats on Big Q doesn't do it a second time.' The man walked over to a sideboard, opened the top drawer and took out a weapon. Shannon froze, and Bob's blood seemed to stand still in his veins.

'I'll pay it back! I swear!'

Big Q attached a silencer to his pistol, unmoved, and Bob clutched the arms of the chair in desperation, pleading with Shannon.

'Help me, Shannon! Tell him I'll pay it back! Tell him I'll never do it again! I . . . I . . . please, Shannon! Please!' His eyes were filled with panic. Sweat began to drip from his forehead. Shannon avoided his look, and was silent. She knew that she couldn't help him. Big Q turned around and circled Bob's chair several times, completely at ease. His voice was neither nervous nor angry, it sounded hoarse and impersonal.

'That wasn't very clever of you, Bob. You should have known not to mess with Big Q.'

'I'll pay it back. I'll pay it back, I promise!' stammered the eighteen-year-old, shaking all over. 'I know I've cocked up. But I promise you, it'll never happen again!'

'That was a deal worth $110,000, my boy,' said Big Q calmly. 'And you have botched it up. Zeppelin is a good customer, and I can't afford to have a boy like you stealing from my best customers. Do you understand?' He stopped in front of Bob, who was ghostly pale and close to tears.

'Give me a chance,' he whispered with quivering lips, 'just one chance! Please!' Big Q raised his weapon, and aimed at Bob's forehead.

'Please!' pleaded Bob.

Big Q pulled the trigger.

Twice.

Bob didn't make a sound as the deadly bullets found their target. He hung in the chair with open mouth and dismayed eyes staring vacantly ahead. Big Q called out a name, and the two muscular, black-clothed men who had accompanied them on their journey appeared in the doorway.

'Take him away,' he ordered, unscrewing the weapon and calmly returning it to the top drawer. The men carried out the dead boy without comment, and Big Q turned to Shannon, sitting rooted to her chair.

'In future, be more careful in your choice of partner.' He nodded to her, polite but cold. 'Let's sit down for lunch. It will be served shortly.'

Shannon got up and followed Big Q to the table without turning back for another look.

The table was set for two.

12

The shadow of death

'On the floor! Everybody on the floor!' roared Shannon, her gun pointed at the three customers in the jewellery shop. It was a sticky summer's day, three o'clock in the afternoon. The customers, an elderly married couple and a finely dressed gentleman with glasses, almost had a heart attack when they saw the young girl with her dyed mane of hair storming into the shop wielding a weapon. The elderly woman clutched her husband, letting out a soft cry.

'Shut it, lady!' growled Shannon. 'On the floor! One move, and you're dead!'

The people did exactly as the girl ordered, while Robby threw a bag to the sales assistant behind the counter.

'Come on, put the money in there!'

Fingers shaking, the woman opened the till and filled the bag with all the money that was there. Her face was as pale as a ghost, and she couldn't manage a sound. The younger man on the floor started to move, whereupon Shannon kicked him brutally in the face with her pointed boots, breaking not only his glasses but also his nose.

'I said don't move, is that clear?' While she kept the customers in check, her brother concentrated on the sales assistant.

'And now open the showcases!' he ordered.

'I . . . I don't have the key here,' stammered the woman, but Robby shoved his weapon even closer under her nose and said: 'Oh no? I'll count to three: one . . .'

The woman thought again. Hastily she reached for a little key and opened the sliding glass door of one of the display cases.

'That's better,' Robby smiled. 'Now, everything in the bag. But quickly, we're in a bit of a hurry.'

The attack didn't even take three minutes. Robby threw the bag over his shoulder, and the pair headed for the hills. As soon as they sat on their motorbikes they heard the sirens of a police car howling up behind them. Cops. That was just what they needed. Either someone had happened to spot them running out of the shop and had been suspicious, or the sales assistant had pressed a hidden button during the attack and so alerted the police. In any case, the brother and sister had no intention of getting caught, and put their foot down.

The police car took up the chase. A shot whistled just past Shannon's leather jacket. Shannon looked at Robby, and they accelerated. But the police were hard on their heels, and a second shot just winged past her upper body. Shannon nodded to Robby and just before the next junction they suddenly turned hard right. At that moment, Shannon felt a sharp pain in her right knee. She took no notice of it, and sped on. They crossed a children's playground and turned into a narrow alleyway, only just big enough for their motorbikes.

'We've left them for dead!' shouted Robby triumphantly, as they reached the next crossing. But he had rejoiced too quickly. They hadn't even gone another kilometre when another police vehicle turned out from a side street. It had obviously been radioed, and the high-speed chase carried on mercilessly. This time it was considerably more difficult to shake off the pursuers, but eventually they boldly crossed a wide lane of oncoming traffic, drove down a steep slope and stopped, breathless, under the concrete pillar of a viaduct.

'Probably better if we leave the motorbikes here and grab ourselves a car,' Robby suggested. Shannon agreed. She swung off the bike, but as soon as her right leg touched the ground it collapsed like a broken match. A hellish pain shot through her knee, and only now did Shannon notice her blood-soaked jeans.

'It's my knee,' she said through gritted teeth. Robby helped her up and put her arm over his shoulder.

'Come on. You've just got to make it to the crossroads. We'll get a car there.' And that was exactly what they did. Robby tore open the door of the first car that stopped at the lights, forcing the driver out at gunpoint. Shannon dragged herself on to the passenger seat, and they drove off. Robby pushed the bag with the loot over to Shannon.

'I think it was worth it, little sis,' he said, pleased, as Shannon opened the bag and rummaged through all the money and jewellery.

'It's definitely worth a fortune,' she agreed, fishing out a gold chain. 'Look at that. We'll easily get a thousand for it. Or this ring here, look!'

'You're better off hiding the stuff until we're out of the city.'

Shannon threw the bag on to the back seat, gasping out a few swear words to try and vent her pain.

'A winger?' asked Robby.

'It damn well hurts for just a winger,' groaned Shannon, and held her knee tight. Only recently the police had shot her in the left leg in another chase, and Robby had operated on the leg himself to get the bullet out.

'I think the bullet has smashed the whole kneecap,' said Shannon, making an effort to be brave. 'This is probably a case for Dr Johnson.'

'That bad?' asked Robby. Half a year had passed since their last visit to Dr Johnson. Even though the doctor had assured them of his help, they hadn't taken him up on it so far. A Jaguar didn't recognise things like pain, and seeking out a doctor was a sign of weakness. Something very serious had to happen for a Jaguar voluntarily to seek out a doctor.

'It's no winger,' said Shannon, and tried to move her leg, without success. 'You won't get this bullet out with the knife, Robby. It's in pretty deep. Damn it.' She swore again.

'So you really want to go to Dr Johnson?'

'Yes, Robby.'

'Okay. But first we've got to make sure the loot is safe. I'm not walking into the doctor's surgery with a bag full of money and jewellery.'

'Done,' agreed Shannon, forcing a little smile. 'Hey, brother. It's fun pinching stuff with you.'

'You're a pretty tough cookie,' said Robby. 'I wouldn't have kicked that man so hard in the mouth.'

'You're far too soft, Robby. That's your problem. If someone attacks you, what'll you do then?'

'The man didn't attack you.'

'But he could have done.'

'He was lying unarmed on the ground, Shannon. He nearly wet himself with fear. And you broke his nose.'

'He can count himself lucky that I didn't finish him off,' growled Shannon. Robby looked over at his sister. His face was full of concern.

'You've changed, Shannon,' he said quietly.

They travelled to Robby's home, he hid the bag with the

loot under a heap of clothes in his room, and then they set off for Dr Johnson's.

The secretary behind the counter nearly fainted when she saw the pair.

'Just don't panic,' grinned Robby, 'it's an emergency, so *no* appointment. Tell the doc he's got visitors.' With that they staggered past the woman in the direction of the consultation room. Shannon was overcome by a strange feeling as she hobbled along the white corridor. The last time there had been five of them, she thought. And now, half a year on, only three of these five were still alive. Bob had been finished off by Big Q a month ago, and Rick . . .

She didn't want to recall it. She had been there when he threw himself out of the fourth floor window. She had watched him do it. She had stood next to him as he did it. And she hadn't stopped him, had even promised him that she would do it too. But she hadn't. Had been too big a coward. Rick had jumped to his death, and she was still alive. They had agreed to kill themselves together, had smoked hash together, opened the window in the fourth floor together. And then he had jumped out, just like that, as if he were a bird, and she stood at the window and watched him do it, just like that. And when he hit the ground and a crowd of people gathered around him, she lost her nerve.

The next thing she could remember was the sound of the handcuffs snapping around her wrists when the police stormed the room and threw themselves on her. They dragged her to the police station, took her finger prints, noted her personal details. They thought it was murder. They thought she had pushed Rick out of the window. Shannon didn't try to convince them otherwise. It wouldn't have made any difference. Rick was dead, and she should have been too. She didn't feel guilty for his death, but she felt bad that she was still alive herself. She was released a day after being taken into custody. Insufficient evidence, they said. But perhaps Big Q also pulled some strings. He had already paid for quite a few of them to be released before then.

That was a week ago. But now it all seemed so unreal, as if it had only been a bad dream, one among the innumerable memories that she had already suppressed.

If someone had asked her why she tried to kill herself, she wouldn't have been able to give an answer. She couldn't give an answer for anything any more. Life was just as absurd as death. Everything was absurd – her decisions, her feelings, the way she thought. Nothing made any sense in her life, and she didn't even care in the least that this was the case. Robby was right: she had changed. It didn't bother her any more if she was violent, if she killed people or let them die. It had become a sort of lifestyle – yes, it struck her as the most normal thing in the world. It didn't have any effect on her any more when someone died before her very eyes. She had seen Bob die, she had seen Rick die, and it was as if her eyes had got used to it.

They entered the consultation room, and again Shannon found herself taken back half a year, saw the two Jaguars in front of her, so real that it was as if they had risen from the dead. She saw Bob holding his weapon to his hostage's temple and threatening the doctor with her death. She saw Rick getting more and more nervous and ordering Dr Johnson to get on with his examination. The scene was so real that she thought she could reach out and touch them, and only Dr Johnson's voice brought her back to the present.

'Shannon? What have you done this time?'

The images from her memory burst like soap bubbles, and she saw Dr Johnson coming towards her wearing the same white coat and looking just as genuinely concerned as he had done on their first meeting.

'They shot at her,' Robby explained, helping Shannon on to the stretcher, where she sat down with great effort.

'Who shot at her?'

'I don't think you should know that, doc,' said Robby drily. 'We've come for you to take out the bullet, nothing more, okay?' Dr Johnson had got the message and didn't ask any further dangerous questions. He could figure out for himself that Shannon hadn't picked up this bullet wound while out for a stroll. Carefully he cut open her right trouser leg and cleaned the bleeding wound.

'Children, children,' he muttered, shaking his head, 'why on earth did you choose such murderous lives for yourselves?'

'Choose?' asked Shannon cynically. 'If you could choose between the gas chamber and the electric chair, which would you choose?'

The doctor didn't answer the question and diverted his concentration back on to cleaning the bullet wound.

'I read about Rick in the newspaper,' he said, all of a sudden. 'I'm sorry.'

Shannon and Robby looked at one another in amazement.

'*What* did you read in the newspaper?'

'His picture was in it – and yours too, Shannon.'

'What?!'

'I remembered you both straight away, of course, and . . .'

'When was that?'

'About a week ago, maybe. I cut out the article and kept it. It's lying on my desk.' Quick as a flash, Robby rushed over to Dr Johnson's writing table and found the article within seconds.

'I can't believe it,' he muttered, and scanned over the report, shaking his head. 'Just listen to this: "The Jaguars are tearing each other to pieces. Yesterday afternoon Rick Blair, 17, fell from a fourth floor window to his death. The police arrested Shannon Ribeiro, 13, who according to eye-witness reports had watched the fatal fall from the same window. Both are members of the Jaguar gang, whose increasingly aggressive crimes have been making the headlines. Shannon Ribeiro is accused of numerous robberies, illegal possession of weapons and drug dealing . . ." '

'Show it here!' Shannon tore the report out of her brother's hands. She was dismayed. 'Who spun them all this material? Where did they get my photo? And my name?'

'Ribeiro. That's no American name.'

'Our father is Brazilian,' explained Robby.

'That's of no interest to the doc,' said Shannon curtly, reprimanding him. She hated being reminded of her father. Since she had been with the Jaguars she had seen him a whole two times. The first time had been in August 1982, one month after she had run away from home. She had taken heroin and cocaine, and was completely out of it when the police picked her up. She heard an unfamiliar voice, someone put her hands behind her back and she was led away. She was so stupefied by the effect of the drugs that she only took in the events as if from behind a veil, and couldn't remember anything afterwards. Not until she felt Dad's violent beatings did she realise that she had been brought home. Of course, she broke away again at the first opportunity and went back to the street.

The second and final time that she saw her father was a year ago now. She had smoked an overdose of crack and had lost consciousness in the park behind the Catholic church. Two police officers found her and brought her to Sister Judith in the nearby church. Sister Judith was a good-natured small nun who put much love and self-sacrifice into caring for the poor, and knew her way with drug addicts. She had already tried to help Shannon once by getting her a job with Father Patrick. But after a week Shannon had robbed the till and made off with the takings.

This time Judith asked the girl whether she'd like to try a drug rehabilitation centre. Shannon agreed, and Sister Judith got her a place in the home. The home offered therapy groups, workshops and other useful activities. But Shannon didn't manage to stay clean; she smuggled drugs into the home, and smoked them secretly on the toilet. Eventually her room-mates pulled the plug on her. Because she denied everything she had to have a test done, which showed up clear traces of heroin, cocaine and hashish in her blood. After that, it was clear that Shannon couldn't stay any longer. In response to the question as to where she had got together the money, she claimed her father had given it to her. Just to give an answer. That was a mistake. Her father was contacted straight away to come and discuss his difficult daughter. That was the last time she had seen him. He would not be reconciled with her criminal life and her drug habit, but did at least manage not to beat her in the presence of the therapists. Only his eyes reflected his real thoughts, thoughts which Shannon knew all too well, and she was relieved that after his convincing performance he marched away again.

'Do your parents actually know what's going on here?' Dr Johnson asked while examining the shot knee and shaking his head.

'Take a guess,' Robby answered sarcastically. 'Our mother's supposed to be somewhere in Japan, and our father's building up his career.'

'They should be made to take responsibility,' said the doctor. 'Every child has the right to a family.'

'Family,' muttered Shannon ironically. A word that could have represented so much warmth and safety, for her it was simply an empty promise, a word without meaning, without any relevance to her life. Only once had this word won any importance for her. That was when Sister Judith found her a place in a young family after the failed attempt in the home. That would be her last chance to get her life back in order, she said. Sister Judith really had meant well, and Tim and Marie Donovan were really quite all right and did their best to make Shannon feel happy with them. They bought her new clothes and shoes, played baseball with her on the street, took her to the swimming pool, to parties. They made a touching effort to give Shannon everything that had been missing in her young life. They wanted to give her a home, a family. But after three months Shannon returned to the Jaguars. The call of the wild life was stronger, and nobody could beat it, not Sister Judith, not the Donovans, not Dr Johnson, not even Shannon herself. She had sold her life to the devil and she had to serve him. That was her fate. And even if she destroyed herself in the process, she still wouldn't fight against it.

Dr Johnson examined her knee and decided it would have to be operated on. He didn't even try to have Shannon taken to hospital for the operation, instead preparing everything himself.

'Ribeiro is no common name here,' he said suddenly while he was anaesthetising Shannon's knee. 'I think there's a professor at the university by that name. There was a report recently in the newspaper about one of his new research projects. Francisco Ribeiro is his name.'

Shannon swore on hearing the name.

'Research at the university!' she growled. 'Well, well – he's started something new! They should write about how he used to "research" his children at home.'

'He's your father?'

Shannon threw Robby a warning glance and said, without

letting her brother out of her sight: 'Do we look as if we had an IT professor for a father?'

'I didn't say anything about IT,' countered the doctor bluntly.

The three all caught each other's eyes, and there was a short embarrassed pause. They all stayed silent, even though they each knew that what had been said should not have slipped out. The matter was too delicate, for all parties. And it was better not to follow it any further. Shannon crumpled up the newspaper article and threw it to the ground.

'Forget what was in there, doc. Forget our names, and stop sticking your nose into things that don't concern you – for your own good.' Shannon looked at the doctor menacingly. 'And now take the damned bullet out of my leg once and for all!'

A few weeks after Dr Johnson had operated on her knee, Shannon and Robby drove out to Lake Erie. It was the beginning of October, a mild day, the sky deep blue and cloudless. The light breeze had tempted lots of sailors out on to the lake. People were walking along the shore, a glider slipped noiselessly through the air, birds were twittering in the tops of the majestic trees that lined the shore. It was one of those days when everything in the world seemed to be fine.

Robby had brought along his guitar. They sat on the grass right next to the shore and he began to play a few tunes. Shannon watched him from the side, and once more she had to admit to herself that her brother meant more to her than she could ever have actually told him. She had saved his life once, and she would do it again and again, because he was the only thing she had in this world. Not even her love for Peggy was as strong as the bond between her and Robby. He was a part of her, and she was a part of him. Their friendship was precious, indestructible, and there was nothing that could have separated them from one another. Nothing.

At least that was what Shannon thought . . .

'I've written you a song,' said Robby after a while.

'Really?' said Shannon, surprised.

'I wrote it when you were in custody. I was afraid they'd keep you in there.' He looked sadly into the distance and plucked a few chords. The wind stroked softly through his long brown hair. His voice sounded serious and melancholy when he began to sing.

> Little sister, do you love me?
> Little sister, can you understand who I am?
> I have no place to go.
> I would die for you, even if you didn't know.
> Little sister, do you love me?
> Little sister, can you understand what I am?
> I am no one, even though I play this game.
> I love you so, and I will never let you go.
> And little sister, in case I should die one day,
> Then I just ask you one thing:
> Don't ever, ever cry!
> Because little sister, for me you are
> The only reason for living.
> Oh, little sister, I love you so!
> Little sister, I love you so!

He let the tune slowly play itself out and waited for Shannon's comment. She had found the song strangely touching. But she didn't know why.

'And? Do you like it?'

'Why do you sing about dying?'

Robby shrugged his shoulders. 'Don't know. Intuition.'

'You're not planning to . . .' She didn't finish her thought.

He had been close to taking his own life once too, and Shannon had reproached him heavily for it, and then, when she had been a hair's breadth away from throwing herself out of the window with Rick, it was Robby's turn afterwards to give her what for. He found the thought of losing his little sister through suicide unbearable, and Shannon felt exactly the same about her brother. They had promised each other never again to do something so stupid, come what may.

'Don't worry, little sis,' Robby reassured her, 'I'm not going to do anything stupid. Who'd look after you if I did?' He pinched her cheek. 'But all the same, you're not allowed to cry if something happens to me.'

She pushed him playfully aside. 'Stop your rubbish now once and for all. It'll bring bad luck.'

He fished out his necklace from under his pullover and closed his fist around the green stone. 'We'll always be together,' he said mysteriously, looking deep into Shannon's dark eyes. 'You must never forget that, little sister.'

And then, two weeks later, it happened. It was a Friday near the end of October. Shannon would never forget this day. The sky was clouded over with grey-black clouds. She and her brother had pumped themselves full of drugs and were thundering through Cleveland on two stolen motorbikes. A lorry appeared before them. One of the back doors swung open and a few packages fell out on to the street. Robby and Shannon thought this was funny, and started slaloming around the packages. The lorry braked suddenly. The lorry driver had probably seen the packages in his wing mirror and wanted to retrieve them.

Disaster struck for Robby. He drove full speed into the stationary vehicle, his motorbike slipping under the lorry and leaving him motionless on the ground. The whole thing didn't even take three seconds. Shannon instinctively wanted to propel herself after him, but she lost control of the motorbike and it began to skid, veering off right across the lane, and she fell down the grass verge. Apart from a few bumps and bruises she was unharmed, and immediately scrambled back up the slope to see what had happened to her brother.

Several car drivers who had witnessed the accident had already got out and rushed over to the scene. The lorry driver was there as well, holding his hands over his mouth in dismay. One of the drivers spontaneously began to direct the traffic; another ran to his car to contact the emergency services. A third went up to Shannon, and asked her if everything was all right. She nodded as if in a trance.

'Are you two together?'

'He's my brother,' she answered softly.

'Would you like to go over to him?'

'Is he . . . ?'

'I don't know. The ambulance will be here any moment now. Are you really okay?'

'Leave me alone,' mumbled Shannon. She sat on the crash barrier and stared without expression at the accident scene. She didn't make any attempt to fool herself. She had seen the crash. He wouldn't survive it. She had lost him.

'Robby,' she whispered repeatedly, 'Robby.' She saw a lifeless body lying on the asphalt in the middle of all the people. She heard his voice, she heard the song he had written for her. She heard it right up close to her ear, and it almost broke her heart.

And little sister, in case I should die one day,
Then I just ask you one thing:
Don't ever, ever cry!
Because little sister, for me you are
The only reason for living.

A lump rose in her throat. She swallowed. No, she wouldn't cry. She had promised him, and she had promised herself that time as well. She could have screamed. Screamed out loud. But she didn't do it. She just looked at her brother from a distance and knew that she had just lost the most precious thing she had ever had: Robby. She cursed the motorbike that had disobeyed her. She had steered left to die with her brother. She hadn't wanted to live any more once she saw his brutal collision, but an invisible force had violently steered right and destroyed her plan. And she didn't understand why. Why hadn't she jumped out of the window with Rick? Why didn't Big Q put a bullet in her head like he did Bob? Why had the police only shot her in the knee, and not the heart? Why did she have to stay alive when everybody else died? What terrible force had sentenced her to live, even though she longed for nothing more than to put an end to this nightmare once and for all? What was the point of carrying on living?

We'll always be together. You must never forget that, little sister.

She took out the leather chain from under her leather jacket and held the blue stone in her shaking fist, not letting her brother out of her sight.

If we both wear these stones and think of one another, we'll be together for eternity.

She could hear his words so clearly, as if Robby were sitting right next to her on the crash barrier. She had clung on to his belief, as if it were her own. She had thought there must definitely be something in it if her brother said so. Together for eternity. It had sounded so convincing, but now, as she sat on the crash barrier and saw him lying motionless on the asphalt, his words suddenly seemed to lose all their force, and they were mere words, nothing more than words, empty promises that were of no comfort to her.

The ambulance appeared, sirens howling. Ambulance men in white clothes sprang out and knelt down next to Robby. Shannon watched the scene with pounding heart, and when she saw one of the men coming away from the group and over to her with a concerned expression, she knew what it meant. Robby was dead.

Dead.

And nothing would bring him back to life. Not even the blue stone he claimed was his soul. It was over. Robby was dead, dead like the blue stone that had never lived. She tore it from her neck and threw it to the ground. The she turned around and ran down the verge.

'Hey, girl! Stay here! Come back! Hey!' She heard the man calling out after her, but she ignored him. She couldn't wait until the police came. And she didn't want to watch them carrying her dead brother away. Perhaps she might have cried then. And she didn't want that. Even when she could hardly hold back the tears. Even when she was more desperate now than ever in her life before. Even when she felt as small and miserable and alone as a thirteen-year-old girl can possibly feel.

She had lost her brother, she had lost her best friend. And she had lost a piece of herself.

She wandered aimlessly through the streets of Cleveland until the first heavy drops of rain began to fall. Her thoughts shrank down to one single word that ran constantly through her head:

Robby.

She forgot the time. And the rain that was pelting down on her with increasing vigour.

Robby, that was the only thing she could think of.

Robby.

He had left her.

And she had never felt more alone.
She had stopped living.

13

His eyes

She didn't recognise him at first. He was a bit taller. But otherwise he had hardly changed over the three years or so. He had the same pale, freckled face and the same blond hair. She stood with Terry in front of the school building, waiting for a boy who owed them money. They were only going to intimidate him a little, tickle him with the knife until he wet himself with fear. They sat on the low wall beside the entrance and watched the schoolchildren spilling out at the end of the day's lessons.

And then she suddenly saw him. He just appeared in front of her, guitar slung over his shoulder, rather surprised to see her.

'Shannon?'

'Nicolas?'

He smiled at her. 'Hi, Shannon. What are *you* doing here?'

'Get lost, squirt,' she growled, even though he was at least as tall as her, as well as a year older. 'And don't start off on any of that Jesus stuff again.'

'You haven't forgotten about it then,' Nicolas was happy to note.

'Forgotten about what?'

'That Jesus loves you.'

Shannon jumped up, grabbed him directly by the collar and flicked her knife.

'Listen up, Nicolas. Say that name just once more, and I'll slit your throat.' She glared menacingly at the boy, but he remained incredibly calm as he returned her gaze. Terry rushed to Shannon's aid and placed his hand on her shoulder.

'Problem?'

Shannon closed her knife and let Nicolas go.

'No,' she said, keeping her eyes fixed on him. 'I think we understand each other.'

Nicolas decided against any further comments and ran off. Shannon scowled after him.

'Who was that?' asked Terry.

'A Jesus-freak,' answered Shannon. 'He annoyed me enough when I went to school here. He was always telling me that Jesus loves me and all that rubbish.'

'So now you go for his throat?'

Shannon flashed her eyes in irritation at Terry. 'I hate the guy. His goody-goody speeches drive me mad, you get me? If I could just smash his face in . . .'

Terry cracked his knuckles. 'Right now?'

'No,' Shannon shook her head. 'Maybe we'll drum up some of the gang and all teach him a lesson together. Tomorrow or the day after.'

'I'm in.'

'I'd like to see if he doesn't quit going on about this Jesus when he feels the fist of the Jaguars.'

Back in the gang's hideout, Shannon gathered a few of her people around her, and asked who was up for a little bit of scrapping. There was no shortage of volunteers. Shannon chose five battle-hungry gang members, and two days later they grouped together at the nearby McDonald's just before school was out. It was an icy cold November day. They were all wearing gloves, woollen caps and several jumpers each under their black leather jackets with the notorious jaguar on the back. They warmed themselves up with whisky, passing the bottle wordlessly from one to the other as they waited for their unsuspecting victim.

They didn't have to wait long. Less than a quarter of an hour after their arrival Nicolas appeared between the houses, his schoolbooks tucked under his arm, coming unsuspectingly towards them. Shannon gave a sign to two of the members of her troupe, and they walked past the boy on the other side of the street, cutting him off from behind. She herself waited for him on the pavement, her legs firmly apart and her arms folded.

'Hello, Nicolas! Great to see you again!'

Nicolas stopped short a few metres away from her and glanced quickly around. He seemed to realise that it was a trap. Shannon smirked.

'Hey, guys! Look, it's the Jesus-freak!' Three burly gang members appeared beside her, and now Nicolas knew for certain what was going on. He turned on his heels and tried to run back down the street, but two Jaguars blocked his way. He tried to escape by making a run diagonally to the right, but again he was blocked. The Jaguars were sealing off all the escape-routes, and the circle was closing in on him. There was no way out. He was in the merciless hands of his enemies. A Jaguar dealt him a hard blow to the chest, winding him and sending him stumbling backwards on to the ground. His school things were scattered all over the asphalt.

Shannon kicked him right in the face with her boot. His lips burst open. Blood ran from his nose.

'Well, what do you say? Does your Jesus still love me now?'

A burly Jaguar picked him up from the ground, and together they attacked the defenceless boy from all sides, punching and kicking him and showering him with filthy language about Jesus and God. One of them spat in his face and smirked: 'They did that to your Jesus too.' Another one dealt him such a heavy blow to his right arm that you could hear the sound of the bone breaking.

'They didn't do that to your Jesus!' he added in cruel amusement as Nicolas gave a howl of pain.

Shannon dealt him a hook to the chin, and he fell to the ground, where he lay slumped in a heap. Shannon took her gun from her belt and pointed it at his head. The five Jaguars moved away from Nicolas and waited for Shannon to pull the trigger and put an end to the scrap. Nicolas, with great effort, pulled himself to a sitting position and, gasping with pain and exhaustion, looked up at her. He didn't say a word. He simply looked at her with those big innocent eyes that seemed utterly clear of even the slightest spark of malice or tiniest trace of fear.

Shannon couldn't understand what was going on in there. Those were no ordinary human eyes that caught her own, they were the gentlest eyes she had ever seen. If there was a loving God then he must have such eyes. If Jesus really did exist, then that was how he would look at her.

She couldn't withstand Nicolas' gaze, and lowered the revolver in shame. She felt really rotten. She had already taken aim at plenty of people, and with chilling brutality she had already shot plenty of kids in battles. She had never hesitated to kill. But this time she couldn't manage it. It just wasn't possible. She couldn't do it. There was something there that was stronger than she was.

'Come on,' she mumbled, embarrassed, 'let's leave him. I think he's had enough.'

Nicolas collapsed and lay unconscious. Shannon nodded to her boys, and they marched off. She looked back again. A woman ran over to Nicolas from the other side of the road and knelt down next to him. Shannon turned away. She had hoped for a victory. She had thought it would fill her with a feeling of satisfaction if she beat up this boy. She had thought that with every strike it would be like hitting out at God in his place, letting out her anger on this God who supposedly loved her so much and yet had taken from her the one person she loved the most: her brother, Robby.

But now, as Nicolas lay unconscious on the ground, she felt that she was the one who had been beaten. Those eyes. Those eyes were what had beaten her. How could he just look at her like that? She had hit him, and he . . . he had looked at her silently with those eyes, with those warm, truly concerned eyes, concerned not for himself, no, but rather for her . . . It bordered on magic. And it was a magic which wouldn't loosen its grip on Shannon. Those eyes. Those green, clear eyes in his blood-smeared face. She couldn't get them out of her mind. They were burning themselves in, deep into her soul, deep down into the very depths of her loss.

When they came back to the factory, Peggy threw her arms around her immediately. 'Hi, Shannon. I missed you so.' She bit Shannon's ear-lobe and kissed her softly on the cheek.

Shannon slipped out of her embrace. 'Not now, Peggy.'

'What's wrong with you? Don't you love me any more?'

'Quit talking about love!' shouted Shannon angrily. 'You don't know a thing about it!'

Peggy drew back in surprise. 'Hey, Shannon. Cool it. I know

that the thing with Robby is pretty heavy, but life goes on, even without him . . .'

'I don't want to hear another thing about it, okay?!' She almost screamed it out, clenching her fists nervously, and stamped off.

An hour later one of Big Q's people rang and told Shannon of a big deal which would be pulled off in a few days' time. Shannon took note of it, but her thoughts were elsewhere.

In the following days she was fairly rough and unresponsive towards everyone. She went out on the street, and if somebody bumped against her purely by accident she went for them with her fists, or even pulled out her knife. She was aggressive and tetchy and yet at the same time indifferent and cold. Nobody from the Jaguars dared come too close to her. Even the most innocent of remarks made her explode. The last traces of humanity within her were banished by her total lack of morals. Life was simply senseless.

A day before the big deal Shannon couldn't take it any longer, and she returned to the school alone, in the vicinity of where she had left Nicolas lying unconscious on the ground. She had to see him. She wanted to find out if the mysterious magic in his eyes had finally died away. She wanted to make sure he had learned his lesson and finally realised that this Jesus couldn't love a person like her. She sat on the low wall in front of the school building and waited. The bell rang and the students spilled noisily out of the building. Shannon looked out for Nicolas as discreetly as possible, and for a moment she even thought he wouldn't come. But he did, and when she saw him she began to feel rather uncomfortable. He was limping. His right arm was in a sling, there were several stitches near the left corner of his mouth, and the right half of his face was swollen and shimmered a violet colour. She sank her head and suddenly hoped he would pass by and not see her. But he had already seen her and was making his way directly over to her.

'Hi, Shannon,' he said, and she wished the ground would swallow her up. But instead she raised her head challengingly and gave the fourteen-year-old a contemptuous look, from head to toe.

'Have you finally realised how pathetic your God is?'

Nicolas tried to smile, but the stitches in the corner of his mouth prevented him from doing so. 'You can do what you want with me, Shannon,' he said, 'it doesn't change my God one little bit. What I said still stands: Jesus loves you.' He looked into her eyes, but she avoided his look, got up and left quickly without saying another word. Those eyes. They hadn't changed. They had looked at her again with the same sparkle, with the same incomprehensible, endless peace which was far beyond her understanding. Those eyes! They nearly drove her mad. And then those words.

Jesus loves you.

She didn't want to hear it any more. She couldn't stand it any longer. They were only words! Nothing more than words! Meaningless, with no effect, simply words.

Nothing more.

Just words.

14

In the hole

It was an icy cold, starry night. It had snowed the whole day long, and although most of the snow on Cleveland's streets had already been stamped into a dirty wet mush, there were still a few isolated patches where it lay white and untouched, lighting up the night a little. Shannon and Terry were sitting in the heated front compartment of the stolen delivery truck, smoking a joint and waiting for their customer to come. A building site formed the ghostly backdrop to the scene. It was a big deal. In the loading area of the vehicle nailed boxes contained numerous kilos of heroin and cocaine, and over 500 kilograms of hashish, altogether worth well over a million dollars. The customer was a drug dealer from Detroit. Shannon couldn't remember ever having pulled off a bigger deal. If Big Q paid them the usual 15 per cent for this transaction, they would cream off drugs to the value of $250,000 for the Jaguars. Naturally, every deal carried a great risk, but with a profit of 15 per cent it was well worth taking it on. Up until now everything had always gone well, and this million dollar deal would also pass off smoothly, Shannon was sure of it.

She had shot heroin, not so much that she hung around with a foaming mouth like a half-dead fly, but just enough to be still in complete control of her mental faculties. She couldn't do anything without drugs. She needed her daily kick in order to get through a normal day, and she needed large quantities in order to feel any effect. Terry looked at the clock. Everything had been arranged for midnight, but it was already seven minutes past.

'Where's he got to, then?' said Terry, nervously voicing his thoughts. 'He should have been here long ago.'

'He'll come,' said Shannon, and took a deep drag from her hashish cigarette. 'He'd be pretty dumb to let this delivery get away.'

'I don't know,' muttered Terry. 'I don't like it. This kind of business doesn't tolerate any delays.'

'Wait it out.'

'You've got balls. If the police have got wind of it, we're done for.'

'What have we got a guard on duty for? You can trust Billy.' Billy was thirteen years old, small and unnoticeable, quick as a hare and an extremely sharp observer. He even seemed to have eyes in the back of his head, and that was exactly why Shannon had posted him as sentry for this deal.

'All the same,' said Terry. 'It's not just *one* kilo in the back of this truck. Do you know how long you get for drug dealing? Two to four years. And with my list of sins you can slap on another few years for free. And not just in the young offenders' unit. I'm already eighteen.'

'Then act like it and shut your mouth. He'll come.' Two more minutes passed, and suddenly a boy on a bicycle turned up out of the darkness. Perhaps about ten years old, he was pedalling for all he was worth.

'Who's *that*, then?'

'Haven't a clue. I'll go and have a look.' Shannon got out, stood in front of the truck and waited. Her breath turned into a white fog in the cold air. She frowned at the boy drawing closer. Something wasn't right, she could sense it. When the boy had drawn level with her, he shoved a little white note into her hand, swung out right and disappeared along a narrow gravel path between the building site barracks. She opened the paper, and her suspicions were confirmed. 'Warning, trap!' was written in large print on the note. Shannon didn't know who the boy was. But that wasn't important. Billy had probably roped him in so as not to risk his own neck. Crafty boy. Shannon climbed rapidly back into the passenger seat and thrust the note under Terry's nose.

'Come on, let's beat it!' Terry turned the key in the ignition, but the engine didn't start. He cursed and tried again. On the fourth attempt it kicked in, and Terry put his foot to the floor. At that very moment, the headlights of an oncoming vehicle flicked on. Terry swore, and tore the wheel around. They were in a dead end, and the only means of escape was an open field to the left. But today didn't seem to be their lucky day. The delivery truck got stuck in the small ditch between road and field, and they had to flee on foot, each taking a different direction. As they did so, the warning shouts of police officers rang out on the air and then shots began to tear through the night. Terry raced across the field. Shannon went to take the same route as the boy on the bicycle, but in the darkness she failed to notice a rusty iron fence lying on the ground, caught her foot in it and fell. Before she could work herself free somebody had grabbed her roughly by the neck.

'Not so quickly, son!'

Shannon hit out wildly, as far as was possible in her unfortunate position, but the police officer dealt her a blow with his rubber baton, momentarily stunning her. The handcuffs snapped shut, and when the man turned her on to her back he said in amazement: 'Well, would you look at that? It's just a girl!'

Shannon spat at him.

'And a very wild girl, at that!' said the police officer, pulling her up violently. 'Don't worry. The young offenders' unit will soon beat the bad manners out of you.'

The young offenders' unit was a huge complex, grey, dead and intimidating. Shannon was accompanied by two police officers, and when the heavy door locked shut behind her she was overcome by a strange feeling of dread. The bare walls silently welcomed her. Even the air smelled of loneliness, and the guards seemed unmotivated and apathetic. So this was going to be her new home, she thought. She shivered at the very thought of it.

Terry had been lucky. His fast long legs had saved him. The idea of spending many years behind bars had probably lent him wings. In any case the police officers hadn't caught him. Shannon didn't know whether they'd been tipped off, and if so, by whom. She only knew that Big Q would be pretty angry about the botched deal. And he wouldn't rest until he was able to interrogate the sneak and personally blow his brains out. Big Q didn't let anyone get away unpunished who had caused trouble, and certainly not when a million dollars were in question!

But would the drugs boss at least remember to get her out of prison in the meantime? It was an unwritten law, a type of code of honour between the big fishes and their smaller counterparts that the big ones bought the small ones out of jail. After all, these were the people who risked head and neck for the drug barons, and when the police did catch someone, then it was always the least important pawns in the game and never the people who actually thought out the moves. They skilfully remained in the background, manipulating the whole show over the telephone on their desk. They didn't get their hands dirty, not them. In the eyes of the law they were irreproachable, beyond all doubt, honest citizens, well meaning and socially engaged, and while a few small fish fell into the police's net on one side of town, they, together with their helpers, carried out the really big business over on the other side. They were shrewd and calculating, acting in cold blood. They were the ones in control, and everyone danced to their tune, even the police, without realising it. It was a game in which the big players had nothing to lose and the small ones everything.

Shannon knew perfectly well that she too was only one of the small fish and was of no interest to the police, but she nevertheless hoped that Big Q would help her out of this pickle. He owed her that after everything she had done for him. She didn't want to fester away behind these thick prison walls for ever, that was for sure. Two days in temporary custody at the police station had been enough for her. They had wanted to hit her with a whole host of crimes. She really had committed most of them, but no one could prove anything. And even if they had done – it would have been just like charging a wild animal with tearing at its prey. She was a Jaguar, and a Jaguar didn't go gathering berries, but rather lived for the hunt.

Accompanied by two police officers, Shannon passed through a barred door. This was closed behind her, and while the guard on the other side of her heaved the key out of his belt for the next barred door they were literally sitting in a cage, squashed in between two closed barred doors. Shannon felt oppressed by the walls and the black bars. A Jaguar behind bars, that couldn't be right. The very idea made her mad.

She was presented to a wiry, grumpy-looking man in uniform, sitting behind a desk in a small office and smoking a cigarette. He wore glasses, was bald and had a moustache. One of the men who had accompanied Shannon passed him some papers which he painstakingly read through, wrinkling up his forehead as he did so. He took his time. After all, he had plenty of it. That was his power, and probably the only triumph he could relish. He enjoyed doing it.

'I've seen your picture in the paper,' he said, looking the girl up and down from head to foot. 'Drugs worth a million dollars in the back of the truck. That number's one too big for a simple girl like you. I'd really like to know who your employer is, Shannon Ribeiro. Wouldn't you like to tell me?'

'My boss is the devil,' answered Shannon flatly. 'And when I get out of here, he'll tear each one of you to pieces.'

One of the officers gave her a hefty box around the ears for this comment.

'Listen, Shannon,' said the man behind the desk, leaning forward as he spoke, resting his elbows on the table and placing his hands together without once taking his eyes off the girl. 'You may not have realised it, but you have just found your way into a young offenders' unit. Here inside it doesn't matter what you were outside. In here, everyone's the same – the same food, the same bed, the same discipline. If you don't want any trouble, then you'll stick to the rules.'

Shannon sulked. They haven't got a clue, she thought. Big Q would get her out of here, before she even reached the cell.

The man typed out a protocol on an ancient typewriter, the police officers signed it, removed Shannon's handcuffs, and left. The man passed the girl to a black female prison warden, who brought Shannon first of all to the shower room.

'Here,' she said, pressing a bundle of lumpy clothes, a towel and a piece of soap into her hands, 'you've got two minutes.' The clothes smelled old and used. The trousers were too wide, the t-shirt and the grey pullover too small. All of the clothes were clearly stamped with the name of the prison, probably just to remind the prisoners that they had been completely delivered into the hands of the institution. Shannon found it humiliating to have to wear clothes that had already been worn by hundreds of girls before her. She wouldn't get her own clothes back until the day of her release.

After the unpleasantly short shower she was taken to a bare room with three chairs and wordlessly pushed down on to one of the chairs by the large black warden. When Shannon saw a man coming up to her with a large pair of scissors she tried to get up and run away. But the warden pressed her back down into the chair and held her there with an iron grip around the neck.

'Regulation,' was all she growled.

The man cut off her colourful mane, and with every dyed strand that fell to the concrete a little piece of pride slipped to the floor. The man finished off his work with a small, buzzing machine, and as Shannon ran her hand over the millimetre-long stubble her feelings of self-worth crashed right down into the cellar. She felt naked – naked and exposed. She heard somebody giggling behind her back in the corridor. She turned around and saw the uniformed man standing against the wall, his arms folded, contemplating her with satisfaction.

'Same clothes, same hair style,' he observed with schadenfreude. 'Welcome to the clink, wild cat!'

She would have liked to go for him there and then, but she was held fast by the strong grip of the prison warden. One day I'll get him, she thought, seething with rage.

They went up a staircase, and through a barred window

Shannon looked down into the inner yard. About fifty girls were marching around in a circle, hands behind their backs, heads bowed, same hair style, same clothes. Like in the films, thought Shannon, only with the one small difference that she was now part of it. And this thought was unbearable.

The woman opened a black cell door and pushed Shannon in. It was a bare room with neon lighting, a bunk bed, a little table, toilet and sink. A girl, about sixteen years old, was sitting on the top bunk.

'Hi,' she said, 'I'm Sheila.'

'Shannon,' muttered Shannon, looking around her new home in disgust.

'What are you here for?' asked Sheila.

'Drug dealing,' answered Shannon, 'and you?'

'Prostitution.'

'How long have you been here?'

'A year.'

'I won't stay that long,' said Shannon, psyching herself up. 'A few days at most.'

'That's what they all think,' said Sheila, nodding.

'I have my contacts,' countered Shannon importantly.

Sheila didn't look impressed. 'How often do you think I've heard that one?' she declared coolly.

'You don't believe me?'

'Even if you knew the President of the United States in person – the laws in here are different to the ones out there. How long did you get?'

'I'm only here provisionally.'

'And when's the court case?'

'No idea,' Shannon had to admit. 'Whatever: they can't charge me. They don't have any evidence.'

'Do you think anyone in here asks for evidence?' said Sheila bitterly. 'And even if your case lasts for months, and even if afterwards it turns out you're innocent, as long as you're in the clink, sentenced or not, you're just the same as the rest of us. Same food, same clothes, same bed.' She pointed to the bottom bunk. 'You're sleeping on the bottom.'

Shannon sat down on the thin mattress and inspected the grey woollen blanket folded up neatly at the foot of the bed. It too carried the stamp of the prison.

'What do you do here all day?'

'Nothing,' explained Sheila.

'That much!' muttered Shannon, full of enthusiasm.

'Sometimes there are therapy groups. Or we plod around the inner yard in a circle for hours. That's all. Otherwise they just let us out to eat and to shower. Oh yeah, and once a week you're presented to the prison psychologist and a doctor, and if you're lucky, you might even get a visit. And there are some social workers somewhere, too, who claim to be looking after us and working on getting us out somehow. At least, that was what they promised me a year ago.'

'What's the food like?' asked Shannon.

'Terrible,' said Sheila. 'Tasteless. We get orange juice for breakfast which they must leave lying around for at least a week beforehand so that it tastes bad, and with it sour milk and old bread, just dry bread, nothing else. For lunch there's a sandwich or a watery soup, unseasoned, really unpleasant. And for dinner rice with chicken, every evening the same, the rice a sticky mass and the chicken cooked for so long that it falls apart on the plate as soon as you look at it. Terrible. The grub here is disgusting. Not even a pig would manage to stomach what they give us here.'

'And what's the story with drugs?'

Sheila gave a wave of her hand. 'There are always some girls who manage to smuggle the stuff in. But if you're caught, then that's it. They're strict with anyone who steps out of line at all here. Their favourite pastime is beating up disobedient girls. And if they realise they're not getting anywhere with that, then they stick you in the hole.'

'In the hole?'

'I was never in it myself. But people say, whoever goes there once never forgets it their whole life long.'

'Why?'

'You're better off asking someone who's been there. Most end up there at some time or other.'

'Hmm,' said Shannon, lying down on the mattress. 'Anything else important?'

'No,' said Sheila. 'That's all. The best way to survive is not to provoke anyone and not to let anyone provoke you. Whoever doesn't stand out is left alone.'

That Shannon wouldn't stick to these golden rules was an easy one to call.

She clocked up the first argument that very lunchtime. The soup didn't taste of anything, just as Sheila had said. After the first spoonful Shannon decided to leave the limp brew to one side. A girl of perhaps fifteen sitting opposite her commented mockingly: 'Shall I spit in it for you? Perhaps it'll taste better then.'

Quick as a flash, Shannon leaned over the table, grabbed the girl furiously by the neck, pulled her right over the table, knocking over lots of bowls of soup in the process, and began pummelling her with punches. A few girls moved back in shock; others gave excited wolf whistles, getting up from the benches to watch the fight. Change was always welcome, it gave a new topic for discussion to pass away the long days and even longer nights. Two supervisors stormed over and violently pulled the girls apart.

'She started it!' said the girl, placing the blame on Shannon and wiping the blood from her nose. 'She's new here and thinks she can go around beating people up like out on the street.'

'What's your name?' one of the wardens asked her loudly.

'Shannon,' she growled, not letting the girl out of her sight for a moment. 'Next time I'll scratch your eyes out.'

The warden dealt her a hefty punch in the back. 'That's enough, Shannon! There are rules here! And whoever doesn't stick to them will be punished! No dinner for you!'

'I can do without this sort of grub anyway!'

'And no breakfast either!'

Shannon soon got a reputation for being a battle-thirsty beast. Hardly a day went by without her getting into some scrap or other. The slightest comment, any look that she felt was out of order, was enough reason for her to hit out with her fists. Sheila was the only person she got on with, and Sheila was also the one who repeatedly tried somehow to take the heat out of Shannon's burning rage with God and the world. But she didn't succeed. With every day that passed Shannon became increasingly more unpredictable. That was also a result of her drug addiction. Her body and her mind had got so used to consuming cocaine and heroin that when she was deprived of them it was pure horror. Depressive bouts of fear and physical pain were the result: she went boiling hot and freezing cold, suffered from cramps and broke out into a terrible sweat.

She spent her fourteenth birthday silently in the cell, sitting absently on the bed and staring at the empty wall. Christmas was just as grim. A few girls received presents or letters from their families. All Shannon got was another warning for bad behaviour, and she had to go to bed without any supper. There would only have been rice and chicken anyway. There wasn't even any change to the daily menu for Christmas. And why should there be? There was no cause for celebration when you were cooped up between high walls and barred windows.

The only thing that would have given her any pleasure would have been to leave this inhospitable place once and for all. But her hope that somebody outside this bare forgotten world would try to free her faded with every day that passed. She had long since given up asking the supervisors when her court case would take place. Even Big Q had probably long since erased her from his memory. She had been thrown out like a book that was finished with, and she would be left in there until she turned yellow with age. Forgotten, rejected, written off. That was her situation. It was enough to make her sick, just like the daily grub, the pointless marching in the inner yard and the eternally grey faces of both the girls and the wardens.

Shannon had got well used to the beatings of the latter, as well as their threats of confining her to the hole if she didn't improve. She had never taken these threats seriously. For a time she even thought the hole had probably just been made up to intimidate the girls into good behaviour. But one day she got to know what the hole was, and it was even worse than everything she had been told.

It was a Wednesday morning at the beginning of February. They were marching around in a circle in -7° Centigrade and longing for the warmth of the heated cell. With red cheeks and noses, hands frozen stiff, the icy cold cutting its way through their thin clothes, they put one foot in front of the other, each girl in perfect time with the others, and each looking stubbornly at the shoes of the girl in front as they all dragged their way round. Whoever slackened off the pace felt the might of the warden's hard wooden baton, and heftily at that. There was a short break in between, and the girls scattered themselves around the whole yard, gathering in small groups to smoke a cigarette and swap gossip, even if there wasn't really such a thing within those walls.

When Shannon passed a girl called Sandra she noticed a grin on her lips. Sandra was well known among the female division of the young offenders' unit as a 'macho'. The girls fell at her feet and were blown away by her masculinity. But not Shannon. She didn't find masculine girls in the least bit attractive. In her first days with the Jaguars, Jeanette had tried to make a pass at her. But Shannon had quickly realised that she felt much more drawn to tender, caring girls like Peggy than to rabid power-girls like Jeanette. Girls like Jeanette or Sandra never even got a look in as far as she was concerned.

'What are you grinning so stupidly about?' she demanded of Sandra, stopping right in front of her.

Sandra came away from the little group of girls around her and stood casually in front of Shannon. 'I'm sorry, I'm already booked up for this week.'

'With the girls or with the supervisors?'

This remark hit home. It was no secret that there were some wardens who could be bought off. Quite a few girls used their bodies to buy themselves laughable privileges. But implying such a thing of a 'macho' girl like Sandra was an insult.

'I can do without this little game of yours,' countered Sandra, whereupon Shannon responded with a psychological clout around the ears:

'Oh yeah? And where did you get those hormone treatments they found in your cell recently? How long did they have it on with you before getting you the stuff?'

Bull's-eye. Sandra's nostrils flared. 'You pig. Think you're something better, just because they leave you in peace?'

'How do you know that? Did they whisper it into your ear at the last rendezvous?'

'Everyone here knows that you kicked one of them between the legs.'

'A shame you weren't there. I would have done the same to you, just to make sure you're not really a man.'

Sandra dealt her a hefty blow for that. Shannon hit back, and with that a wild scrap was already underway. Shannon – all Jaguar – went for Sandra, tearing her to the ground. The girls came running from all sides to witness the fight first hand. The wardens came storming over as well, as the two girls wrestled on the wet tarmac, fired on by the whistles and shouts of their fellow prisoners.

Shannon quickly won the upper hand, held Sandra down with her knee on her chest and in a blind rage began to strangle her. The shouts died away and a stunned silence took over. This wasn't any normal fight any more. Sandra wriggled like a worm and tried to free herself from Shannon's grip, her hands wide open in sheer panic. But Shannon had no intention of letting go of her throat, and she probably would have killed her if the supervisors hadn't fallen on her with their batons and violently pulled her off.

Sandra lay rasping on the ground, and Shannon covered her head with her hands as the wooden batons mercilessly swiped down on her. She screamed and groaned.

When one of the wardens stood her up, she nearly collapsed right back down again. Her whole body was shaking; it didn't seem to obey her any more, her movements were uncontrolled and disturbed. A few of the girls knelt down next to Sandra and called Shannon every name under the sun they could think of. Others watched the scene, disconcerted, until one of the supervisors shouted at them in reprimand: 'What are you standing around for? Back into the circle! There's nothing more to see here! Show's over. Move yourselves! Come on, come on!'

The girls obeyed.

'And you, Shannon,' said a warden, holding the baton under

her chin, 'are going to the hole. Perhaps *then* you'll learn how to behave here.'

They dragged Shannon across the inner yard, past the girls marching once more in a circle. A few cast a furtive glance over at Shannon, immediately earning a strike from the baton.

'Heads down! The next to look will find themselves in the hole as well!'

Three of them hauled the fourteen-year-old girl into the building, along the corridor, down a staircase, then along a gloomy passage and down another staircase into a cellar that looked just like a dungeon from a history book. A single light bulb lit the room. The atmosphere was damp and musty.

So this was the infamous hole, thought Shannon, and as if he had read her mind, one of the supervisors said grinning: 'Don't count your chickens before they're hatched. This is just the forecourt. The hole is back there.'

One of the men went up to a black iron door, pushed back the lock and opened it. The weak light coming from the bulb wasn't sufficient to light the room beyond. Shannon shuddered. Absolute darkness was waiting for her behind this heavy iron door. So *that* was the hole. She shivered with cold. The supervisors stripped her naked and Shannon was helpless to stop it. They threw her into the jaws of darkness, laughing contemptuously.

'Twenty days of the hole, my sweet! Have fun!' The door fell shut, the bolt was drawn, and night fell, the darkest night imaginable. So *this* was the hole.

She heard the men leaving and their footsteps and voices echoed along the walls. Then it fell nastily silent. Shannon tried to get up. But she couldn't manage it. Her whole naked body was shivering and shaking uncoordinatedly, and it took quite some time for her to get her movements back under control.

The wardens really hadn't spared her this time with their batons. It was actually forbidden to beat the inmates. The girls were meant to have a medical check-up every week so that the authorities could satisfy themselves that they were being handled well. Officially everything in the young offenders' unit was in top shape, and the supervisors made quite an effort to keep up this image. There was always a plausible explanation for a few bruises at the medical check-up, and the more difficult cases unofficially disappeared for a while, at least long enough for the worst wounds to have healed.

Twenty days of the hole. Twenty days without sunlight, twenty days in perfect darkness, not knowing whether it was day or night. Slowly Shannon began to realise why the hole was so feared by everyone and why nobody ever dared mention it, out of fear that they might themselves end up in it. It really was the most horrible, inhumane way to punish someone, and after just a few minutes Shannon already regretted going for Sandra. But now it was too late.

She felt along the wall and established that her concrete cage was no larger than the average bed. The cell was one metre wide, two metres long and one and a half metres high. It stank of excrement and urine. The floor and the walls were cold and seemed to want to collapse in on her from all sides. Just how she was supposed to survive in here for twenty days was beyond her. It was as if she had been buried alive. She remembered a boy from her gang whom she really had buried alive because he had taken flight in a battle against Rage. And cowards were personally put to death in her gang. She remembered his face filled with panic when she had thrown him into the ditch and filled it up with earth. Her heart beat wildly at the thought. The memory alone pulled her throat tight and she felt as if she was choking on it. Whoever digs graves for others . . . Now she herself was lying in one, in the hole, tossed in like an animal, naked, her body aching and her soul bleeding, robbed of all human dignity.

She had become like an animal.

And the devil was laughing down at her in contempt.

15

On the brink of madness

'Food!' They threw her the plate and bottle as if she were a dog.

'How long to go?' asked Shannon hoarsely.

'Five days!'

The door clanked back shut, the footsteps moved away. The fifteen seconds of contact with the outer world were over.

'Five days,' murmured Shannon, and felt around in the darkness for the bottle, 'five days . . . five days . . .' She hastily unscrewed the bottle top with her dirty fingers and quenched her burning thirst. Then she fell hungrily on the food, rice and chicken, just as tasteless and unappetising as ever, and wolfed it down, not leaving a single grain of rice on the plate.

'Five days . . . five days . . .' Most of the food had fallen down on the floor into her own excrement. But her hunger was too great simply to leave it there. In the last fifteen days only three times had she got her teeth into something. On the first occasion, she only ate what had stayed on the plate, but by the second time her raging hunger had brought her to eat what had fallen next to the plate as well.

'Five days . . . five days . . .' She repeated the words like a magic formula as she gnawed on a bone she had salvaged from the floor.

'Five days . . . a quarter of twenty . . . three quarters over . . . just five days to go . . .' She had lost all sense of time. She didn't know whether it was day or night, whether outside the sun was shining or if it was snowing. All she knew was that she had another five days to stay in the hole, five long, torturous days in the midst of rats, cockroaches and her own excrement, shut out of human society for another eternity, another eternity on the brink of madness.

Most of them go through it, Sheila had said, and Shannon didn't doubt it. She herself was in the process of going through it. Sometimes she stroked her own arms and repeated the same words over and over again, thousands of times.

'That's me . . . that's me . . . that's me . . .' Again and again, as if she had to convince herself that she still existed.

And then finally it was over. After five meals and three weeks of mental torture in complete darkness the iron door opened and Shannon was let out. She crept out of her cave on all fours like a starved wolf, stinking, smeared from head to foot with excrement, skeletal, the hate that over the twenty days had eaten its way right inside her shining from her dark eyes. The light from the naked bulb hurt her eyes. She couldn't make out a thing, just silhouettes and shadows and the voices of the wardens who had thrown her into this hole 480 hours ago with mocking laughter.

'Well, Shannon, are you going to be a good girl now?'

That was too much. It was the straw that broke the camel's back. Head down and screaming wildly Shannon went for the first silhouette she set eyes upon and started beating it with her fists. The supervisors fell on her.

'I think our wild cat wants to go back into the hole!' one of them cried.

'How about another twenty days?'

With these words Shannon's fuse finally burned right through. Back into the hole? They couldn't do that to her! She wouldn't survive it! She lost it, completely. Like a rabid animal she began snorting madly and hitting out all around her.

'No! No! I don't want to go back into the hole! I don't want to back there ever again!!!' She screeched and screamed, bit and scratched, and it took a well-aimed hook to the chin to put her out of action long enough for the men to overpower her and carry her up to the washroom covered in a blanket. The same fat black woman who had received her on her first day in the young offenders' unit four months ago pressed the same lumpy clothes, towel and piece of soap into her hand and waited at the door, her arms folded.

'You have four minutes,' she said generously. 'The psychiatrist wants to see you.'

'But I don't want to see him,' muttered Shannon angrily to herself. She didn't want to see any psychiatrist who would draw conclusions about her personality from her behaviour, as if it were a matter of writing a weather report. She wanted only one thing: her freedom – and no one would give her that.

It was as she had feared. The enlightened psychiatrist sat behind a tidy desk in his comfy leather chair, looked at her with his psychologically schooled eye through his incredibly intellectual glasses, and had already formed his opinion about her before a single word had been spoken. They should lock *him* up in the hole for twenty days and then examine *his* wits afterwards, thought Shannon. He wouldn't last a day in there, not a single damn day. And then he would go to court, or to the White House, or to the UN, and charge the young offenders' unit with a breach of human rights. With one of the top lawyers, of course. And with the whole press behind him. And the whole land would break out in uproar, and the whole thing would be investigated and the staff of all the young offenders' units would be changed and the old supervisors would be held responsible and put in prison. And the poor psychiatrist who had spent a day in the hole would be declared a national hero and awarded the Nobel Peace Prize.

'Shannon, how do you feel today?' The stupid question brought Shannon back to reality.

'Crap,' she said honestly. The psychiatrist keenly noted a few essential words on his pad. What did he know about life, thought Shannon. Nice clean fingernails, a Mercedes parked in front of the thick prison walls, a nice little holiday home out in the countryside. How could such a person think himself fit to judge other people, just because he'd spent a few years at university?

'Why do you feel . . . bad today?'

'Crap,' Shannon corrected him.

'Yes,' said the psychiatrist, and scribbled on his pad. 'So why?'

'Would you like to change places with me and find out the answer for yourself?'

The psychiatrist kept on keenly writing.

'What do you particularly fancy now?' he asked, firing another question at her. 'What would you really like to do now?'

'Smash your gob in.'

The psychiatrist cleared his throat, but didn't otherwise show any visible signs of discomfort, instead noting everything conscientiously in his notepad. That was his job, after all.

'What are you afraid of?'

'Certainly not of you. But if you like I can set a few Jaguars on your throat and then we'll see who's afraid of who here.'

The psychiatrist made his notes as keenly as if he were

collecting points for it. Then he reached into his waistcoat pocket and offered Shannon a chewing gum.

'Would you like a gum?'

'Only if you don't make a note of it in your stupid notebook.'

'Why? Does it make you nervous?'

'*You* make me nervous.'

'Why?'

She hated this question. She hated this psychiatrist with his sly look and gold pen.

'Because you do nothing but ask me smart questions that you don't want to know the answers to!' She was irritated. She was fed up. She wanted to get out of here. 'Why don't you ask me if I like it here!' she shouted, raging. 'Ask me if I want to get out of here! I'll tell you: I *do* want to get out of here! I want to live my life at last! But you're not interested in that. You just want to analyse me, categorise me and file me away, just like all the others. As far as you're concerned I'm nothing more than a crazy, dangerous creature who has to be kept away from society for as long as possible!'

The psychiatrist adjusted his glasses and carried on writing.

'Yes, be sure to note all that down!' screeched Shannon, beside herself with rage over this laughable hearing, and got up. 'And when you've noted everything on your clean white paper, get your fat ass off that leather chair, have a stroll outside and think about what you're going to cook for dinner this evening. Know what I'm going to eat this evening? I'll tell you. Rice and chicken. And tomorrow too. And the next day! But you don't give a damn about that! You won't be here this evening to eat rice and chicken! That's not your job! And that's why I hate you! I *hate* you!' She gave the desk a hefty kick and with one movement of her hand wiped the telephone and a few papers from the table, and for the first time the psychiatrist stopped writing and looked up, pretty shocked. Two wardens stormed in, grabbed Shannon and forced her back down on to the wooden chair.

'I hate you! I hate you all!' screamed Shannon, raging with anger. The psychiatrist got a hold on himself again, wrote and wrote, and after a few minutes tried a few more questions. Only the strong hands of the wardens stopped Shannon from going for the man behind the desk and scratching his face to pieces. Eventually the psychiatrist took off his glasses, wiped his forehead in exhaustion, passed his notes to one of the wardens and pronounced his sober judgement.

'Take this message to the director, and tell him that this girl is mentally ill, crazy, disturbed, has a very disturbed view of the world.' And then he started spouting medical jargon. Shannon thought she picked up terms like 'psychopathic', 'paranoid' and 'psychotic'.

She flared up again. 'You see, just what I said. You're good at rubber-stamping things. You should get a job at the post office, it's even easier to stamp things there!'

The psychiatrist didn't take any further notice of Shannon. As far as he was concerned, the case was closed. *Psychopathic, paranoid, psychotic*, something like that.

'Tell the director this girl should be admitted to a mental hospital.'

'You dog! You miserable dog!' shouted Shannon. 'I'll tear you to pieces when I get out of here, I swear I will!' She was lifted up violently by the wardens.

'Have her admitted today if possible,' she heard the psychiatrist's voice behind her as they went through the doorway. 'This girl is capable of anything . . . Next, please . . .'

Shannon shot like an arrow out of the white hospital bed and knocked the glass with the medicine out of the male nurse's hand.

'I'm not taking that stuff any more! I'm not taking it any more! I'll kill you! I'll kill you all!!!'

'Sister, call for help!' cried the nurse, desperately trying to defend himself against the girl's attack. In a few seconds, hurried steps could be heard on the polished floor and a whole crowd of carers appeared in the entrance to the ward. Four of them overpowered the fourteen-year-old and gave her an injection. She fell still immediately.

'Just look at that. That crazy girl bit me in the hand.' The male nurse showed the others the wound. The imprint of Shannon's teeth could clearly be seen on his hand.

'She's mad. We're best off putting her in the padded cell for a few days. Perhaps she'll calm down then.'

The suggestion was taken up. They put Shannon into a straitjacket and brought her to a white room that looked like an upholstered capsule without any windows. There was a neon light on the ceiling, bathing the room in a harsh cold light. Shannon didn't try to defend herself. The injection had tamed her like a little pussy cat, and her arms were so bound up that she couldn't have done anything even if she'd wanted to. So this, she thought, was the mental home's 'hole', a slightly more comfortable version for the mentally insane, as she was now classified. She sat herself down in a corner.

Psychopathic, paranoid, psychotic. The psychiatrist had said it. And he probably hadn't been so far off. Whoever was put in a straitjacket and confined to a padded cell had to be crazy. How long had she been here? Two months? Or four? She had stopped counting the days. Every day she spent here was one day too many. Every morning when she opened her eyes and saw the white sterile walls of her room she wished this nightmare would finally be over. Her body was crying out for drugs, her soul for freedom. She wanted to kill the whole staff. She just couldn't take it any more. It was driving her insane.

And that was just what everyone thought she was.

All day long they pumped her full of strong medication. When she had one of her fits, they tied her down to the bed and gave her electric shocks in order to stimulate her brain, as they put it. There were also conversation groups. Shannon particularly disliked these. They asked such idiotic questions, and you couldn't even crack a joke. It was awful, and she seriously asked herself whether she would ever get out of this white hell.

She spent four days in the padded cell. They spoon-fed her like a small child. It was humiliating. And there was no end to this mental whipping in sight. Everyone had probably long since forgotten that a Shannon Ribeiro existed who had been shoved away in the loony bin, and she would spend an eternity between these white walls and white nurses, longing for her release. Her cry for help wouldn't even get as far as the wall, never mind any further. Her case was no longer for the eyes of the public. And at some point it would be put to rest in a dead file. No one would notice her death, it wouldn't change a thing. Her life wasn't worth being reported. It had never existed. It was meaningless.

Meaningless?

Her life was anything other than meaningless. Her life had made the headlines! But Shannon didn't know anything about that, nor that she had these headlines to thank for her freedom, until one morning a nurse laid her own clothes on the bed and smilingly announced:

'Get changed, Shannon. You're being collected.'

'Collected? By who?'

'I don't know,' said the nurse. ' But I was told you were being collected.'

Shannon was distrustful. 'Am I going back to prison?'

The sister shook her head. 'No. You're free, Shannon. There's a man waiting outside to collect you.'

'Does that mean I can go?'

'Yes. That's exactly what it means.'

'I'm free?'

'Yes.'

'Don't have to go back to prison?'

'No.'

Shannon had to digest this incredible news. Free. She was free! How could such a thing be possible? And who was the man who was collecting her? Big Q? No, Big Q would never dare come here. If Big Q had wanted to buy her out, he would have done it a long time ago. But who else could it be? She didn't have a clue, didn't think any longer about it either, because at the moment only one thing counted: she was free! After four long months in the young offenders' unit and another even longer four months in the mental home – free. She couldn't grasp it. Free!

She didn't know whom she had to thank for her freedom, but she was eternally grateful to him, whoever he was. He had saved her life.

Free!

Quick as a flash, she slipped into her boots, jeans, t-shirt and black leather jacket. It was an indescribable feeling, being able to get back into her own clothes after eight months. She had never felt so good in them. She wouldn't have changed them for any gold-decorated dress in the world. It was the scent of freedom that hung on her clothes. The scent of her life. She had risen from the dead.

She marched with her head held high past the nurses and carers, feeling like a queen. She could feel the scepticism in their looks as to how on earth it was possible to let such an insane girl back out among the human race. It amused her. She was even tempted to give them the finger, just to shock them a little more, but generously she let it be. She was free. That was the only thing she could think of as she burst through the entrance door and scampered out into the hot sunny July day like a playful squirrel. It was a wonderful day, just made to steal a motorbike and drive it out to Lake Erie. The Jaguars would be stunned. She was back. Her inner clock began to tick again. She could have shouted out loud for joy.

But then she looked up, and saw him. Her heart nearly stood still.

He was standing there.

The man who was supposed to collect her.

The man who had saved her life.

It was her father.

16

Brazil

'Hello, Shannon.'

Shannon didn't say anything. She stood at the entrance, not moving.

'Hey, aren't you going to greet your dad? I got you out of here, after all.'

'Hi,' muttered Shannon reluctantly.

'Get in,' he said, nodding to his car. 'I'm not planning to grow roots here.' He hadn't changed. Was just as stiff and impersonal as the last time they had met, almost two years ago now, that time when she was in the drugs home that Sister Judith had found for her. Shannon hadn't expected to ever see him again, at least certainly not under these circumstances. Whatever had brought him to get her out of the mental home was a mystery to her. She went up to him hesitantly, opened the door without comment and sat in the passenger seat. Her father started the engine.

'Wasn't easy to get you out of there,' he said.

'Why did you do it, then?'

'You're my daughter.'

That hadn't ever been a reason for him to even lift a finger for her before, thought Shannon. There was a catch to this story, but she didn't know what.

'I'm flying to Miami, Florida, on business tomorrow. You can come along, if you want.'

Something was definitely wrong here. Something or other.

'I've been invited as a guest speaker to an IT conference. I turned up some astounding research results over the last year. I'm to talk about them in Miami.'

'Hmm,' said Shannon, uninterested. He *really* hadn't changed. Thought only of himself and his career. How *she* had got on over the last months probably didn't interest him at all. He could at the very least have asked, just for politeness' sake. But there was no place for her in his world. It had always been like that. And that was why she was surprised that he had got her out of the loony bin. That just didn't fit the bill. Not for him. He didn't waste his time on hopeless cases like her. That wasn't his style. He only ever looked after his own interests. Expenditure and profit had to add up. He called it calculated risk. Collecting a crazy girl from the mental home wasn't exactly a lucrative business proposition. There was something behind all this, and she would find out what.

'How long are you staying in Miami?'

'Two days. Then we'll fly back again.'

Two days, considered Shannon. She had never been to Miami, but she knew one thing: there was good heroin there. She could get some for her and the Jaguars. And her father was paying for the flight. That wasn't a bad deal. She couldn't let such an opportunity slip away.

'Okay, I'll come,' said Shannon.

★ ★ ★

On the very same day she sought out the Jaguars. When she pushed open the heavy door of the factory hall, most of the kids were on their drug trips and didn't take any notice of her. It was a strange feeling, being back. She scrambled over a few empty beer bottles, and nearly fell over a couple making out. When she looked more closely, it was as if she'd been struck by lightning.

'Peggy?'

Peggy looked up.

'Shannon!' she cried, shocked, pushing a strand of hair out of her pale face. The girl lying next to her sat up as well. It was Jeanette. Who was the most surprised of the three was hard to say.

Shannon looked into Peggy's big green eyes and didn't know how she should react to this situation. She felt betrayed, cheated on. Peggy looked ashamed and desperately sought for words to explain something which had already explained itself.

'I thought you weren't coming back,' she stammered, at a loss.

'I was just comforting her a little,' contributed Jeanette, and put her hand on Peggy's shoulder. 'Surely you didn't expect Peggy to wait around a whole year for you?'

'Eight months,' growled Shannon. 'It was eight lousy months. But I'm back now.' She looked at Peggy. 'You're not going to swap me for this hussy, are you?'

Peggy was torn in two. The old passion for Shannon sparkled in her eyes, but Jeanette's hand clawed unmistakably at her shoulder. She wasn't able to utter a sound.

'You can't win them all,' grinned Jeanette. 'Tough luck.'

Shannon considered whether she should thump Jeanette one, but pulled herself together and let out her anger on Peggy instead.

'In a few days you'll regret your decision and wish you were back in my arms. But then it'll be too late. It's over between us.' And with that she stamped off, head high, not turning around once. She didn't want Peggy or Jeanette to see just what an effect the whole thing was having on her. A Jaguar didn't recognise weakness. At least Peggy should feel guilty and think that Shannon was easily able to get over the end of their relationship. She should realise what she had just lost. She should suffer a bit. After all, *she* was the one who had been unfaithful, so she should bear the consequences.

Shannon went to the president's office and burst in on a war meeting. Paul, Terry and a boy she couldn't remember were there. Paul looked thin and worn down. With black rings under his eyes and sunken-in cheeks, he looked like an old man. Terry was wearing a patch over his right eye, and the third boy, a strong titan of a guy, at least six foot six and with sharp facial features, had a bandage wrapped around his left hand. The boys stared at the girl for a few seconds, their mouths open, as if she were a ghost.

'Shannon!' cried Terry. 'Did you run away, or did they actually let you out?'

'My old man got me out.'

'I thought he didn't want to have anything more to do with you,' remarked Paul, and a rough cough shook his chest.

'That's what I thought, too,' said Shannon, refusing to go into any more detail and instead coming straight to the point. 'Tomorrow he's flying to Miami and is taking me with him. I thought I could use the opportunity to get us some stuff.'

'How much?' asked Paul, businesslike.

'As much as the Jaguars can afford.'

'You won't botch it up again, I hope.'

'Hey! That wasn't my fault! I've just spent eight months in

the clink for it! Somebody sneaked on us, and if I find out *who*, I'll beat him to a pulp!'

'Not necessary,' said Paul drily, 'Big Q has already done that.'

'Who was it?' asked Shannon.

'One of his own people,' the titan explained. 'The police caught him, and in order to save his own skin he spilled the beans.'

'The pig,' growled Shannon. 'And *I* was the one who copped the whole thing. Big Q could at least have bought me out.'

'Was probably too risky for him this time,' said Terry. 'At any rate, he's punished the guilty party.'

'I hope he died slowly.'

'You know Big Q's methods,' said the titan. 'Quick and discreet.'

'How do you know that?'

'I'm the new war minister.'

'What about Edmond?'

'He is no longer,' said the titan coolly, and Shannon knew what he meant. He had beaten him in battle, just as she had done Johnny. The news took her by surprise, and hurt. She had liked Edmond. Really liked him. He had respected her, hadn't ever been stupid and had a go at her like the other boys. He had seen her as an equal, and that was just what she had valued in him. And now he was dead. It would have to be Edmond.

'Roger is our new war minister, and Billy has taken over your post,' Paul continued to fill her in.

'What do you mean, taken over my post?' said Shannon, surprised. 'What about *me*?'

'Hey, girl. You were behind bars, and we didn't know when you'd get out again.'

'But I'm back now!'

'The drug trade goes through Billy now, okay?' Paul looked

at her in irritation. 'If you want your post back, you'll have to fight for it. You know the rules.'

Shannon was raging. She felt as if she'd been put out to roost.

'I *will* fight for it, you can count on it.'

'Good,' said Paul, 'and now go away. We've still got something to discuss here – between men.'

'And what about Miami?'

'Talk to Billy about it.'

'I need the money by tomorrow evening at the very latest.'

Paul coughed and nodded. 'Like I said, that's Billy's business, not mine.' He nodded to the door. She understood, and left. She was burning inside. She had been away for eight months, just eight months. And everything had changed. Edmond was dead, Billy had taken over her post, Peggy was together with Jeanette – and as for her, she wasn't needed any more. She had been tossed out like an old shoe. Every person is replaceable, and so was she. This realisation hurt. She probably hadn't even been missed, just had her name struck off the Jaguars' list, as if she were nothing more than a few letters on a piece of paper. Nothing more. Just a few letters.

She went through the huge factory hall, and suddenly felt terribly alone. No one took any notice of her. She had become a stranger in her own gang. A girl was sitting on the ground, reeling and spluttering to herself. A boy was overcome by the sudden need to throw up, while his mate sat next to him, uninterested, gabbling senseless rubbish to no one in particular. A girl was examining an open wound on an older boy's leg. A little group was smoking a joint, another one was drinking itself stupid. The same scenes as ever. Some members were dead, other new ones had joined, but the pictures they offered were just the same, as if everything ran in a cursed circle of suffering and death from which there was no escape. Robby had said that life would consist of birth and rebirth. But if the hope in that was to return to this miserable world, then it was a pitiable hope, especially when you had scenes of absolute despair before your very eyes.

It all suddenly struck Shannon as so grim, so disgusting, so senseless – and yet eight months ago it hadn't bothered her at all. But Edmond had still been alive then. And she had still been the intermediary for the drug trade. And Peggy had thrown herself at her feet. Once again she had lost everything that had ever meant anything to her, and nobody seemed to be in the least bothered by it. Everyone just looked out for themselves. Everyone lived for themselves, and everyone snuffed it for themselves. Surrounded by hundreds of Jaguars, Shannon felt she was the loneliest person in the world.

It was a humid Friday afternoon when Shannon boarded the plane in Miami with her father in order to fly back to Cleveland. Everything had worked out excellently. The Jaguars had entrusted her with over $13,200 to buy heroin. And she had bought 600 grams of the best quality and hidden it in her luggage. The trip had been worthwhile.

Her father hadn't got wind of anything. He had left Shannon to her own devices over the two days and concentrated on his talks for the university. They hadn't spoken much in that time. Their conversation had limited itself to only the most necessary of details, and now her father was sitting next to her in the plane and leafing through a newspaper while Shannon observed the comings and goings of the airport ground staff through her window. The kitschy, smiling stewardess demonstrated the safety procedure to the passengers. But Shannon's thoughts were with the Jaguars. Perhaps she'd win back her respect there with this load of heroin, she considered. That was what she hoped, at any rate.

After a while the pilot's voice sounded over the loudspeaker, and Shannon nearly had a heart attack when the pilot named the destination: the flight wasn't going back to Cleveland, as she had thought – rather, it was going to *Brazil*!

Shannon did a dismayed double take and stared at her father.

'Is this some kind of joke? What's going on here?'

'It was the only way to get you to come,' said her father, without even looking up from his newspaper. Shannon tore the paper out of his hand and got up from her seat.

'Let me through. I want to get out!' she snorted, and tried to push past her father. 'I want to go back to Cleveland! I'll scream if you don't let me through!'

'And I'll tell the stewardess you're my daughter, and you have psychological problems.'

'Let me through!'

'Sit down, Shannon!'

'Let me through!!'

A smiling stewardess appeared in the gangway and politely enquired whether she could be of any assistance.

'Yes!' shouted Shannon. 'Get me out of here! I didn't know that this flight was going to Brazil! There's been a mistake! I want to go to Cleveland!' The slim lady smiled uselessly. She had probably never experienced such a situation.

'She's my daughter,' Shannon's father now intervened in order to reassure the stewardess. 'She's terribly afraid of flying, you know.'

'I'm not at all afraid of flying!' Shannon retorted. 'I'm just sitting on the wrong plane, don't you understand? And that's why I want to get out of here!' The stewardess tried hard to retain some semblance of an unforced smile.

'I'm sorry. You can't leave this plane any more. We're taking off in a few minutes. But if you like, I can bring you a glass of water . . .'

'I don't want a glass of water! I want to go to Cleveland!' Shannon nearly screamed it out, and lots of passengers turned around to look at her. The stewardess began to sweat. A steward hurried over to take care of the situation. Shannon looked at the outraged faces of the other passengers, and all of a sudden it shot through her like a bolt of lightning: the heroin! Even if she somehow dramatically managed to get off the plane before take-off, the 600 grams of heroin would fly in the hold to Brazil. And she couldn't return to the Jaguars without the heroin! She was done for. Like a balloon suddenly losing all its air, she slumped back into her seat and fell suddenly silent.

'It's all quite all right,' her father assured the steward. 'She's just not used to flying. Sometimes she loses it.'

'She's a little pale,' the steward observed, and turned to Shannon. 'Do you not feel well?'

Shannon shook her head mechanically. 'It's all right,' she murmured. 'I'm okay now.'

'Shall I bring you a glass of water?'

Another shake of the head.

'She's always like this when she flies. The excitement, you know. She's terribly frightened of flying. But I think she's calmed down now.'

'Let's hope so,' said the steward, frowning. 'Just call us if you need anything.'

'Thank you,' nodded her father, smiling. 'Thank you very much.' He waited until everyone had turned away again, and then looked menacingly at his daughter. 'Don't do that again, all right?' he whispered viciously. 'I'm still your father, whether you like it or not. And I'm going to take you to my parents in Ribeirão Preto, whether you like it or not! Is that clear?'

'I don't want to go to Brazil. What am I supposed to do there?'

'Finally see sense!'

Shannon's heart was beating wildly. She was burning with rage over this unfair trick of her father's. A two-day trip to Miami. He'd worked it all out excellently. And she had completely gone along with it, had thought they would fly back to Cleveland, had trotted along behind him through the departure hall like a good girl, not taking any notice of the black signs with the white writing which could have destroyed his outrageous plan. If only she'd looked! But her thoughts had been elsewhere. She'd been daydreaming. She hadn't read that instead of saying Cleveland the signs had all said São Paulo! She could have kicked herself for her stupidity. But now it was too late.

The aeroplane gathered speed, and as it took off from the ground and the houses shrank down to toy-town size, Shannon felt as if a fist were turning her stomach inside out. So that had been the hitch. That was why her father had fetched her from the mental home. To take her to Brazil. But if he just wanted to get rid of her, why didn't he simply leave her in the loony bin? It didn't add up. There was something fishy in the story.

'Why?' she muttered, and turned to her father. 'Why did you take me out of the asylum?'

'Why? I'm quite happy to let you in on it. Because I had a court case hanging over me because of you, that's why.'

The answer surprised Shannon. And she couldn't make much of it. A court case around his neck? Because of her? That didn't make any sense. Her father filled her in straight away.

'Your case caused a stir. Now the state wants to take away my custody over you. But that's not the deciding point, Shannon. The point is that you and your criminal life set the press on my back. You're amazed, aren't you? Well, there's not too many Ribeiros in Cleveland, and the fact that a university professor should have the same name as a street urchin was like letting blood into a piranha tank as far as the journalists were concerned. They sniffed a big story. They wanted to go public with your case, wanted to ruin my good reputation with it. Journalists know no mercy, not when they've discovered a lead. Their tongues were practically hanging out for the headline: "Professor Ribeiro and his criminal daughter". A real juicy one for the press. I had to buy them out on many occasions to stop them dragging my name through the gutter – and all because of you! You almost had me ruined, Shannon. And so I had to bargain with them. That was why I got you out of the mental home, and that's why I'm taking you back to your grandparents. Because I'm finally sick to the teeth of this whole circus. I won't let anyone ruin my life – not anyone, do you understand?'

Shannon said nothing. So *that* was the catch she had been searching for in vain. She should have known it. This wasn't about her. It was about him. Only ever about him. *His* life was endangered, *his* career, *his* reputation. And it was even supposed to be her fault. That he might actually be responsible for the course her life had taken, he had probably never even dreamed of. He didn't want to hear anything about how he had destroyed *her* life. She was a hindrance to *his* success, and that was why he was taking her to Brazil. She should have known it. She should have known it as soon as she had seen him in front of the mental home. He was calculating, only concerned about looking after his own interests. That was what he was like, Francisco Ribeiro, her father. And she hated him for it. She hated him more than anything else in the world.

Brazil. Ribeirão Preto. Her grandparents. She didn't like the thought of returning there. Five and a half years had passed. Five and a half years since her father had tempted her to the USA. Five and a half years. She'd just been a rebellious child back then, nine years old. Now she was fourteen, and old enough to take care of herself. She wouldn't stay with her grandparents, that much was sure. But she couldn't return to Cleveland any more either, not even if someone paid for her ticket. She had botched it up. Paul would kill her with his own hands if she dared set foot on Jaguars' territory. In her own eyes and in the eyes of the gang she was a traitor. The gang had entrusted her with $13,200 to buy heroin – $13,200! The Jaguars would never ever swallow that her father had simply landed her in it. They would tear her to pieces before she even managed to open her mouth.

But that wasn't the only thing making her head hurt. The far bigger problem waiting for her in just a few hours was the Brazilian customs. If they found the drugs on her, she was done for. It was 600 grams of heroin, after all! Drugs worth $13,200! She felt hot just thinking about it. Her father had got her into a damned sticky situation. Shannon shifted around in her seat uneasily. The tension was almost driving her mad. She could only hope they wouldn't find the stuff. She had a fifty–fifty chance. And the time-bomb quietly began to tick.

The nearer they got to São Paulo, the more nervous Shannon became. Six hundred grams of heroin. They mustn't find it. They'd put her straight back into prison. And this time not just for eight months.

When she walked through customs with her rucksack and sports bag she nearly wet herself in fear. She thought everyone would spot her nervousness from a mile off. She felt as if she were wearing a sign around her neck, clearly visible to everybody: 'Look, drugs!'

She was sweating. Her heart was beating so wildly she thought it would burst. Any moment now they were going to wave her to one side out of the queue, she thought. Any moment now they were going to want to look in her luggage. A fourteen-year-old girl with shaven head and black leather jacket didn't exactly inspire confidence. The customs officials knew the face of a scoundrel when they saw one. That was their job. And Shannon had already heard horror stories about the Brazilian police.

But she came through customs without any problems. A great weight lifted from her heart. Once more, she'd been lucky. She'd got her neck out of the noose one more time.

They travelled to the bus station, and from there took the bus to Ribeirão Preto. The journey took five hours, and they reached the town at eight o'clock in the evening. They didn't say a single thing to each other throughout the whole journey. Shannon knew only one thing: if her father thought she was going to stay with her grandparents like a good little girl, then he had another thing coming, quite another one. She was big enough to look after herself, even in Brazil. At the first opportunity she would disappear, gather a few people together and form a gang. Even if she wasn't going to return to her gang in Cleveland, perhaps never again, she was still a Jaguar, and a Jaguar was no house-trained pussy cat.

The family reunion was warmer than she had expected. Shannon made an effort to scrape together her Portuguese. She'd forgotten most of it over the five and a half years, but nevertheless she more or less managed to make herself understood. The whole clan had assembled to greet her: Grandma, Grandad, Uncle Felipe, Aunt Fernanda, Aunt Carolina, Aunt Sara and her children, Michel, Larissa, Carlos – and Adriano. A strange feeling came over Shannon as she stood in front of her cousin Adriano and shook his hand. It was five and a half years since she had said goodbye to him, five and a half long painful years. An eternity. So much had happened, so much that should never have been allowed to happen. She had changed – and so had Adriano. And yet there was something in their eyes that mysteriously bound them to one another, a deep longing for freedom and peace that was hidden away in the darkest corner of their hearts, recognisable only in the sparkle of their eyes, those mirrors of the soul.

'I didn't forget you, Adriano,' said Shannon.

'I didn't forget you either,' Adriano assured her. They smiled at each other, slightly at a loss, and couldn't find any more words to describe what they were feeling inside. You couldn't pack five and a half years into a few laughable words. And certainly not in front of the whole family.

'Well, my children!' Grandma cried out after everyone had exchanged greetings. She clapped her hands. 'Now we're going to eat! Before the churrasco turns to charcoal on the grill!' She stamped into the house, and the company all followed her into the inner courtyard where various skewered kebabs were hissing over a coal fire. There was rice, beans, salad and a whole selection of alcoholic and soft drinks to go with it. The tinny sound of samba music tinkled from a pocket radio, and soon the entire neighbourhood had gathered in the Ribeiros' back yard. Everyone laughed, danced, ate and sang until late into the night.

It was just as it had been, thought Shannon. Nothing had changed. Only the date – and herself. How often in the USA had she longed for the fiery Brazilian temperament, for the happy parties in her grandparents' back yard, for the scent of the palm tree she had climbed so often as a child. And now that she was back, she suddenly felt so alien, homeless, lost between two cultures, neither of which was really hers. When she had first arrived in the USA, she hadn't felt American; now she no longer felt Brazilian either. It was as if her spirit hadn't yet landed, had instead got lost somewhere between Cleveland and Ribeirão Preto while on the search for her real identity.

'Shannon, do you want one?' Adriano's voice brought her back to reality. He was offering her a cigarette, and on closer inspection Shannon realised that it was a hashish cigarette. She was surprised, but certainly wasn't against the idea. It was about two in the morning, and nearly everyone had retired to bed. Only a few young people were still up, including Adriano and his brothers and sister.

'Where do you get the stuff from?' asked Shannon, as her elder cousin lit her cigarette for her.

'We call him Grándão, the Big One,' Adriano informed her. 'He's the biggest drug dealer in town. He'll sell you whatever you want – grass, cocaine, crack.'

'Heroin too?'

'Heroin? You must be joking.' Adriano grinned. 'We're not in the United States, Shannon, we're in Brazil.'

Shannon sucked the bitter-sweet smoke down into her lungs. 'How can I get in touch with this Grandão?'

'I can take you to him.'

'When?'

'Tomorrow evening?'

'Done,' Shannon nodded. 'I've got something that may interest him.'

'Just watch out, Shannon. Grandão is hard to impress.'

'He'll be impressed by *this*,' said the girl, blowing the smoke into her cousin's face. 'You can count on it.'

The next day was a Saturday. Shannon's father had had a heated discussion about her with Grandma, keeping his real reason for bringing her back to Brazil a secret, of course. As far as he was concerned, he had washed his hands of Shannon, and that very afternoon he hastily took his leave of the family and took the bus to São Paulo. Shannon hoped she would never see him again.

Late in the evening, Adriano collected his cousin on his motorbike to go and meet Grandão. They entered a dingy bar, full of shady characters. Adriano headed for a large, muscular black man, and tapped him on the shoulder. The black man turned around, and critically looked the two of them up and down.

'We'd like to speak to Grandão.'

'About what?'

'Business,' said Shannon.

The black man waved over a second man, and then together they searched the two for weapons. Eventually they led them downstairs into a basement room and told them to wait there. A little later, a scrawny coloured man in his mid-forties entered. He wore a gold chain around his neck and his fingers were decorated with numerous rings; his smooth black hair, combed back over his head, shone under the neon light. So this was Grandão, thought Shannon, the big shot of Ribeirão Preto. Obviously it was easier here to get to the big shots than in the USA. The slim, colourfully clothed man sat down at the table, his hands clasped together, while his black bodyguard stood firm in front of the door.

'What do you want today?' he asked Adriano, not taking any notice of Shannon.

'Nothing,' said Adriano. 'Shannon insisted on talking to you. She's my cousin.'

Grandão's eyes wandered over to the girl. 'If you've got the money, I'll get you anything you want, Shannon. I'll even do you a special deal, seeing as you're Adriano's cousin.'

'I'm not here to buy,' said Shannon. 'I've got a present from the USA for you.'

Grandão began to look curious. 'A present? What kind of present?'

'Something you've never seen before.' She reached into

her jacket pocket and fished out a small, see-through plastic bag filled with a greyish powder. Triumphantly she placed it on the table in front of Grandão, and folded her arms expectantly. The man opened the little packet, frowning. He smelled the powder, took a little pinch between his fingers, and tasted it.

'It's for snorting,' he muttered. 'But it's not cocaine, and it's not crack.'

'Heroin,' Shannon filled him in.

He looked at her in astonishment. Adriano's jaw dropped, equally amazed, and the black muscleman at the door craned his neck in curiosity.

'Heroin?!' repeated Grandão. 'Heroin's only ever made it once to this town.'

'Well, this is the second time, then,' said Shannon with a saucy laugh.

Grandão couldn't believe his eyes.

'Where on earth did you get it?'

'From Miami,' Shannon informed him. 'Best quality. Do you want to see for yourself?' Shannon was well exercised in snorting and shooting heroin, and she took great satisfaction in being one ahead of the biggest drug dealer in Ribeirão Preto. She warmed the powder in foil over a candle, Grandão inhaled the dangerous fumes through a little straw, and was impressed by their narcotic effect.

'And now I'll show you what's *really* good.' She mixed some of the powder with some water until it frothed, sucked it into a needle she'd brought with her, and gave the man a shot. Grandão was enthusiastic.

'How much of the stuff do you have?'

'A bit,' said Shannon vaguely. 'I've brought thirty grams along for you.' Grandão's eyes nearly popped out of his head when Shannon laid the powder on the table.

'An expensive present. How much did you pay for that?'

'Twenty-two dollars per gram.' Her audience didn't believe their ears.

'Are you crazy, Shannon? That's $660!' cried Adriano.

'What do you want for it?' asked Grandão.

'I want to work for you.' For the second time that evening, Shannon managed to surprise her listeners. The drug baron looked hard at the girl.

'Why should I let you do that?'

Shannon played her final trump card, slipped out of her leather jacket and showed Grandão the Jaguars' symbol on her right arm. 'I used to belong to the Jaguars, the most infamous gang in Cleveland, before I came here,' she explained, not without a certain pride. 'Give me a knife, and I'll slit open your bodyguard's stomach before your eyes. Give me a revolver, and I'll kill any man for you without so much as batting an eyelid. I'm not afraid of the police, nor of the clink – I've already been there. I've worked for the biggest drug dealers in Cleveland. I know my stuff.'

Grandão got up and paced around the room, lost in thought. He didn't doubt that Shannon was telling the truth, even if it did sound incredible. This girl seemed even more cold-blooded than most of his own people. And she had experience. And courage. And was without doubt very iron-willed. This girl was made of particularly strong stuff. It would be an interesting move to have her in his business.

'Okay, girl. You're in. Come along tomorrow evening, so that I can introduce you to a few friends. But I'm warning you: don't try to joke around with me. That could be a very expensive mistake, very expensive.'

Shannon nodded. 'I won't disappoint you, Grandão.'

The drug dealer smiled with satisfaction and made a sign to the black man on the door.

'Give Shannon a generous portion of cocaine for her handsome gift.'

He went over to Shannon and clapped her on the shoulder. 'This day will go down in the history of the drug trade. And your name too, Shannon.'

Shannon felt at home in her role. It wasn't so bad after all that her father had brought her to Brazil. The Jaguars had taught her to fight, and she was strong enough now to fight on alone, out on the streets of Brazil. The heroin would open plenty of doors for her and earn her the respect she needed.

A new chapter had begun. A chapter in which she alone decided what was to be done. She was free, free at last to be her own boss. In her pocket were 570 grams of heroin, and in her head was the belief that she could conquer everything and everyone. Nothing could stop her now. The world belonged to her.

17

The encounter

'So, we'll try it again, girl: who's your employer?'

'No one.'

The rubber baton swished down on her mercilessly, and Shannon screamed out. She'd been hung on the parrot perch like a dead pig on a spit. She had been hanging on this metal pole for the last two hours, her hands tied together, her arms pulled over her knees, the pole shoved between her arms and the backs of her knees. It was one of the most infamous methods of torture used by the police to make their suspects confess.

'You don't have to pretend anything with us, Shannon,' said a small, wiry police officer, waving his baton around in front of her face. 'We know that you know more than you want to tell us. We know you're the head of a gang that works for the biggest drug dealer in town. We know that you and your gang are responsible for a number of unexplained crimes, also for a number of murders. Tell us the name of your accomplices, and you're free. Tell us the name of your boss, and we'll let you go.'

'You won't get anything out of me!' Shannon growled from between gritted teeth. The rubber baton hit her right in the middle of her face. She could taste blood on her lips. Another strike knocked her senseless, and everything went black.

It was Thursday 5th June 1988. Two years had passed since Shannon had returned to Brazil. Two years filled with drug dealing, crime and spiritualism. Through her Aunt Sara, who herself was a fortune teller, she got to know Mother Raimunda, a 'holy mother', as she was called. And that was just what she was for Shannon: a mother. And Shannon was her 'holy daughter', as Raimunda called her. The sorceress introduced her to various occult practices, and Shannon wouldn't do anything any more without her agreement and 'blessing'. She drank chicken blood, entered cemeteries backwards in order to show respect to the spirits, sealed pacts with spirits and took part in every ritual that Mother Raimunda recommended. Once she had to lie on the ground, and the woman scattered leaves all over her body to make her immune to all injury.

'I am closing your heart and your mind,' said the witch in a low voice, making strange noises as she did so. 'I am closing your body to knife wounds and bullets, so that no one can kill you.'

For a time, Shannon even lived with the old woman, just as she had moved in with Grandão for a few months. But somehow neither had suited her, and eventually, along with a few other homeless birds, she set up her own home. It was the first *mocó* in Ribeirão Preto – a type of cave, an underground passage which she, along with a few strong boys, had dug out with her own hands. It was a safe hiding place, right in the town centre under an small park. A few loose boards covered the entrance, which they could always skilfully fit back into the flower bed so that no one ever suspected there might be a hidden den underneath. Using the park gardener's tools, they tunnelled through the ground like moles until they had hollowed out a sizeable hole: their home. Admittedly, it wasn't particularly cosy. There were cockroaches and rats, the air was heavy, and it smelled of rubbish and excrement. But Shannon had already lived in other holes and felt quite at home here. They slept in there, took drugs, amused themselves and cooked soup on a small gas stove. Sometimes there were up to twenty people living in the *mocó* – people who had been rejected, persecuted, filled with despair and helplessness and who no longer had a place in this world. These were people whom society had officially 'aborted' because they didn't fit the norm and therefore had no right to live.

'Wakey-wakey!' Shannon heard the voice as if through cotton wool, and then felt cold water being thrown over her. 'We're not finished with you yet.'

Shannon opened her eyes, and saw, standing next to her, the same wiry police officer who had been torturing her with electric shocks and beatings for the last two hours in order to try and squeeze information out of her about the drug trade. A second police officer was sitting on a chair next to him, filing his fingernails.

'The names, girl!' growled the wiry police officer. 'We want the names! Tell us the names!'

Shannon was stubbornly silent. She would never betray her people, never. There was Roberto, Grandão's brother, who was also a drug dealer and for whom she occasionally did business. There was Carioca, a big strong guy from Rio de Janeiro and a professional killer who took orders to finish people off. There was Loira, a seventeen-year-old fair-skinned boy with shoulder-length blond hair who she herself had trained to be a cold-blooded gangster. She spent most of her time with Carioca and Loira. Jefferson joined them later on, and then David, a long-haired guy with green eyes and a constantly sorrowful expression. He had a cobra tattooed on to his right arm. And the sixth member of their gang was Cat. They called him that because he had one green eye and one brown one. He had Japanese facial features, and smuggled in drugs from Colombia. Cat became Shannon's best friend.

'So you're not going to tell us who you work for?' said the police officer, repeating his question for the thousandth time that night.

'I certainly won't tell you, you filthy beast!' spat Shannon, full of contempt, and the next strike on her hands made her roar out in pain.

'We can lock you up if you don't say anything.'

'You don't have any evidence against me,' gasped the sixteen-year-old. 'There's no evidence. You can torture me to death here, I won't tell you a thing, not a thing.'

The police officer on the chair carried on filing his finger-nails apathetically as the rubber baton swiped down on Shannon's body. Then the man waved his colleague over and whispered something into his ear, and at long last they took the girl down from the parrot perch. She collapsed like a dead animal. Her wrists were grazed open by the rope, the backs of her knees hurt, her whole body felt as if it had been attacked by a pneumatic drill. They wrenched Shannon up and led her away in handcuffs, but instead of taking her to the prison cell they sat her on the back seat of a police car and travelled with her to a dingy side street on the edge of town. There they untied her.

'Run!' one of them commanded. A shiver ran down Shannon's back. She knew what that meant. They wanted to shoot her dead like a beast, and then officially claim that she had tried to flee. She knew this macabre little game, and she knew that this time they were intending to play it with her.

Her blood seemed to freeze in her veins. She looked at the two police officers in dismay as they prepared their weapons, as if for a practice shoot. Only this time their target wasn't a dummy; it was a sixteen-year-old girl.

'Run!' ordered the wiry police officer a second time, striking her with the handle of his weapon. She forgot her pain and began to run, knowing that ultimately she didn't stand a chance. She was as good as dead. The police officers would have her flat on the ground before she had reached the first hut, about a hundred metres away. This run would be her last. She was running straight into hell.

The first shot was fired after she'd run about thirty metres. It just missed her. She gritted her teeth and ran on. Another sixty metres to the hut. A second and a third shot tore through the night. They should have hit me ages ago, was the thought that surged through Shannon's head as she raced on, not letting the hut on the right-hand side of the street out of her sight for a moment. Another fifty metres. She was running faster than any sprinter in the Olympic games. Her steroids were the deadly bullets of her enemies, which at any moment could bring her to the ground. Another forty metres to go. A race against death. No way out.

And yet some invisible hand seemed to be directing the bullets away from her, because out of the seven shots fired, not one had them had hit her yet, nor even grazed her. It was bordering on magic. Did Mother Raimunda have something to do with it? Had her ritual with the leaves really made Shannon's body immune to all injury? Another twenty metres. Shannon ran as she had never run before, reaching the hut with her last scrap of strength. Exhausted, she collapsed behind the wooden wall, unable to understand how she had made it. They should have got me – the thought kept shooting through her head – why didn't they get me? There was no explanation for it. Either Mother Raimunda's magic really had protected her, or the police officers had purposely let her escape because they hoped that one day they would catch her with her whole gang. In any case, she was alive. That was all that counted. She was alive. For whatever reason. She had pulled one over on the devil, death and the police. All the same, she waited, heart pounding, until the police officers got back into their car and drove off. Then she gathered herself together and limped back into town.

A week later, Shannon visited her grandparents so that she could have a proper shower and wash her clothes. The family was well accustomed to her trotting in out of the blue, staying a few days and then going back into the jungle of the town. They didn't try to stop the girl. They didn't ask any questions any more. Grandma had only given her granddaughter a dressing-down once, when she had disappeared without trace for several months and then suddenly turned up at the door one day, dirty and smelly, like a homeless street urchin. But then she got used to the idea that Shannon had grown too wild to be tamed now, and let her lead her life as she saw fit. Of course, she hoped that some day her granddaughter might see sense of her own accord.

'Shannon! Great that you're here!' called Aunt Fernanda, when the girl came out of the shower, almost knocking her over with her hug. 'I'd like to introduce you to someone.'

'You're not about to get married, are you?'

The aunt laughed. 'No. He's a pastor, and he leads our service.'

'Service?'

'We meet every week in our sitting room.'

'Are you crazy? Pastor, service – in Grandma's sitting room? What's all this about?'

'Come along. You have to get to know Cesar. And our group.'

'I couldn't give two hoots about your group and this Cesar guy. What's that got to do with me?'

'Are you afraid?'

'I'm not afraid of anyone!'

'So come along, then.'

Aunt Fernanda had beaten her niece with her own words, and Shannon had no other choice than to follow her meekly into the sitting room, so as not to look a coward. A pastor! What interest had she in a pastor! She'd shake his hand quickly and then beat it. A service! That wasn't for her. And she was amazed Aunt Fernanda was involved in such a thing. That wasn't her style. Fernanda was sold on mysticism, yoga, that sort of thing. The last time Shannon had visited her family, maybe about three months ago now, Fernanda had still been into doing her transcendental exercises, and in the sitting room at that. And now she was suddenly getting all excited about a pastor holding a service in that very same room! There had to be something very strange going on there.

Shannon glanced sceptically over Fernanda's shoulder. The small sitting room was crowded with people. Over forty people had pushed their way into the room. Some were standing, others were sitting on chairs and armchairs, still more, due to the lack of space, had found a spot on the floor. They were all talking excitedly with each other. Fernanda waved a young man over. He looked just over thirty, was thin, wore jeans and a white t-shirt and had short frizzy hair. All in all nothing special, average to dull. He came over to them, smiling, and Fernanda beamed as she presented Shannon to him.

'Shannon, this is Cesar. Cesar, this is my niece, Shannon.'

'Oh,' said the man, stretching out his hand to her. 'So you're Shannon. Your aunt has already told me lots about you.'

It sounded as if he already knew all about her, and Shannon didn't like this thought one little bit.

'What nice things have you been telling him about me, then?' she asked her aunt cuttingly, with a rather reproachful undertone. She shook the pastor's hand briefly, and their eyes met. Shannon jumped inwardly as she looked into his light brown eyes. It was as if she'd already seen those eyes before, and she even knew where. In Cleveland. In front of the school. The eyes were the same, the look, the way they shone. This wasn't Nicolas standing in front of her. No, this was Cesar here, an unexceptional pastor. But he was looking at her with Nicolas' eyes, and that confused her. Greatly.

'Are you staying for the service?' the pastor asked welcomingly.

Shannon shook her head. 'I'm not too hot on your God. I belong to the opposition, so to speak.'

'And do you like it with the opposition?'

She had wanted to intimidate him, but she clearly hadn't succeeded. 'You know what? That's sod all of your business, pastor. I serve *my* god in *my* way, and you serve *your* God in *your* way. So we'll leave it at that, okay?'

Shannon wanted to turn away at that, but the pastor wasn't letting her dispense with him so easily.

'I used to think just like you. I smoked hashish and felt as cool as you like. But God had mercy on me, and now he needs me to help other people who are going through the same thing as I once did.'

Shannon shook her head. 'You can't impress me with that, pastor. You haven't a clue about real life.'

'Whoever doesn't know Jesus doesn't know real life. Jesus himself says: I *am* life.'

This pastor with his pious spouting was slowly beginning to get on her nerves. 'Shut up with all that rubbish. I'm not the right person for it. Didn't I tell you: I don't believe in this Jesus of yours.'

'But he believes in *you*. And I'm sure Jesus still has plenty of things in store for you.'

Shannon smiled pityingly and turned away. A pure waste of time even listening to such stuff. Jesus still has plenty of things in store for you – what absolute rubbish! What difference did this Jesus make to life? This pastor would have to find himself another fool to fall for his idiotic prattling. She didn't want to have anything to do with it.

'You can always change sides,' she heard the pastor calling out after her. And then he said something which had the same explosive effect on her as a bomb: 'Jesus loves you, Shannon.'

What she really wanted to do was whip out her weapon and shove it under the pastor's nose. But she didn't. There they were again, those words that were always turning up, those words that had almost cost Nicolas his life and nearly driven her mad. Those words that seemed to have followed her since she was ten and had never really loosened their grip on her. But why did she get so nervous whenever she heard them? They were only words, after all. Empty words. Harmless words, that couldn't have any influence on her life! So why all the fuss? *Jesus loves you*. There was no love in this world. And this Jesus didn't exist, either. All just stupid talk. But all the same . . . a strange power emanated from these words, something that shook her up inside. And she didn't know why.

She went into her room, sat on her bed, took her weapon out from under her t-shirt and weighed it thoughtfully in her hand. Love. No one should speak to her about love. People understood only *one* language, and that was the language of violence. Shannon hadn't experienced anything else in her whole life. And whoever claimed that there was love and understanding in this world was a hypocrite. Or off his trolley.

She heard singing coming from the room. Was her aunt singing along? Shannon couldn't understand why Aunt Fernanda had swapped her meditative yoga exercises for this little group. What did she get out of this boring little lot of people? And why was she so excited about Cesar? He wasn't anything special. There had to be something behind it, and Shannon wanted to get to the bottom of this mysterious power these people seemed to possess. There had to be a catch in it all somewhere.

Shannon hid her weapon under the bed, went back and stood discreetly in a corner where nobody noticed her. Aunt Fernanda was sitting in the front row. The pastor was standing at the front with a large black Bible in his hand from which he was reading out loud.

'If I speak in the tongues of men and of angels, but have not love, I am only a resounding gong or a clanging cymbal. If I have the gift of prophecy and can fathom all mysteries and all knowledge, and if I have a faith that can move mountains, but have not love, I am nothing. If I give all I possess to the poor and surrender my body to the flames, but have not love, I gain nothing. Love is patient, love is kind. It does not envy, it does not boast, it is not proud. It is not rude, it is not self-seeking, it is not easily angered, it keeps no record of wrongs. Love does not delight in evil but rejoices with the truth. It always protects, always trusts, always hopes, always perseveres.'

Shannon listened to the words in amazement. They were clear, simple and comprehensible; they spoke out to the audience, sounding soft and warm. *Love.*

Cesar looked up from his Bible and spoke to the small assembly. His face was beaming. 'My friends,' he said, 'God's love is powerful and endless. Paul, who wrote to the Corinthians with these words, was Jesus' greatest enemy. He persecuted Jesus, he hated the Christians to the core, he whipped them, put them in prison and killed them. And God did not hold it against him. Because God is love, and love is not resentful! Paul knows what he's talking about. He called himself the lowliest of all sinners. He was present when they stoned Stephen. And he took pleasure in his death. Just imagine that: he enjoyed watching someone die – someone who had done nothing other than believe in Jesus Christ and display his belief in public. But the people closed their ears to Stephen's words, fell upon him and dragged him out of the city to stone him. And Paul, then known as Saul, minded the murderers' clothes.'

Shannon jumped on hearing these words. Nicolas! She could see him in front of her, falling to the ground amid the kicks and punches of the Jaguars. She had the scene so clearly in front of her that it was as if it had only happened a few days ago. And she saw herself pointing her weapon to his forehead, ready to kill him. And he had just looked up at her with those big gentle eyes of his. She shuddered at the thought.

Shannon hung on Cesar's every word as he continued: 'God would have had every reason for letting this bloodthirsty Paul die for all of his atrocious acts. But he did the opposite. He did not meet him with anger, but rather with endless love, and asked him only one question: "Why are you persecuting me? I am Jesus, and you are persecuting Jesus!" '

The pastor looked into the assembly, and Shannon hid behind the door so that he couldn't see her.

'What side are *you* on? Are you one of Jesus' followers, or one of his persecutors? Whatever side you're on, God loves you. He loves you with all your flaws. He loves you so much that he gave his only Son so that *you*, if you believe in him, will not be lost, but rather will be granted eternal life. And if God's love is strong enough to convert Paul, a persecutor of

Christians, indeed even a murderer of Christians, then it is strong enough to convert any person, without exception. Of this I am convinced.'

Shannon was listening attentively to his description. Something had her transfixed. Not necessarily *what* Cesar said was making an impression on her: rather, it was *how* he said it. His words seemed to spring straight from his heart. He spoke with incredible devotion and the strongest of convictions. She couldn't say why, but this man seemed somehow incredibly genuine, incredibly fascinating. She stayed until the end, and after the final prayer she observed how everyone hugged each other and began talking to one another. They were like one big family where everyone was interested in everyone else and nobody was left on the sidelines. And Shannon realised that she felt incredibly comfortable in the presence of these people. Some of them even spoke to her and asked her if this was her first time here and how she had liked the service. She didn't let much slip about herself, but nevertheless felt that the people were taking her seriously and including her in their community.

That made an impression. Up until now everyone had always met her with distrust, and one of her basic principles was not to trust anyone in the slightest either, not after she had been exploited and betrayed her whole life long. But these people didn't seem to fit the bill; instead, they seemed genuinely interested in her. For the first time in her life she had the impression of being accepted just as she was. For the first time in years she had the impression of being human again. And even if she didn't understand how this could be possible, she was nevertheless determined to unearth these people's secret.

18

The turnaround

'I'll tell Cesar.'

'You'll do no such thing.'

'I have to. It's not right, what we're doing.'

'Who says so?'

'The Bible.'

'The Bible. Now all of a sudden you come at me with the Bible after we've been amusing ourselves quite happily for the last three months. You should have thought earlier about just how exactly you wanted to stick to Christian morals.'

It was 14th October 1993. Shannon was pacing the room nervously. Josiane, a pretty, slim girl with frizzy black hair, was sitting on her bed and biting her fingernails. Josiane was twenty, a year younger than Shannon and a member of Cesar's church. The two girls had got to know one another there, and out of a normal friendship had grown a sexual relationship. Of course, no one knew about it; it would have caused a scandal in the church and been a bitter disappointment for Cesar after everything he had done for Shannon over the last five years.

And that was why he mustn't find out about it, not under any circumstances.

'It's better if we tell the truth,' ventured Josiane again.

'Better for who? Do you think I want to lose face in front of Cesar and everyone else?' countered Shannon, not standing still for a moment. 'I've been rejected in my life often enough now.'

'I shouldn't have got involved in all this,' murmured Josiane, ashamed. 'What we've done is simply wrong in God's eyes.'

'I thought God was pure love.'

'God's love for his people has nothing to do with sex. And he despises homosexuality. God destroyed whole cities in the Old Testament for it.'

'A strange way of loving people.'

'There's a line: God loves the sinner,' Josiane explained, 'but he despises the sin.'

'Well that's a good one,' roared Shannon. 'You know all about God's opinions. And to make sure that this loving God doesn't strike you down in a bolt of wrath, you want to blow the whistle on us to Cesar.'

'He'll find out about it some day anyway. He found out about the drugs.'

'You haven't a clue!' Shannon berated her, shaking her head and gesticulating wildly. 'For you, it's probably nothing more than a little slip-up. You ask your God for forgiveness, and that's the end of it. My reality looks a bit different, Josiane. I wasn't born into the church. From the age of ten onwards I had to fend for myself. I had my first homoerotic dream at the age of eight. And I took my first shot of heroin at the age of ten. And then you come along and think we can simply make everything be all right again!'

Shannon stopped in front of the window, ran her hand through her shoulder-length curly hair and stared out into the distance. She had tried. She had really tried to change her lifestyle. Several times. But she had failed. She couldn't do it. Cesar had constantly motivated her to try and change direction, for five whole years.

'You can't carry on like this, Shannon,' he had said again and again. 'You want to solve all your problems yourself, in your own way. But you can't pull yourself out of the swamp by grabbing on to your own hair, that's just not possible. Only God can solve your problems, Shannon, and in his way. You need Jesus. You won't get out of all this without him.'

She thought he was a pious fool. He meant well with her, sure. And she thought it was nice of him to go to such bother for her. But this Jesus wasn't for her. Perhaps he could solve other people's problems, but hers were too great and too complicated for him. She was convinced of it. For five years she swung constantly back and forth, from heaven to hell, from prison and drug dealing to the church. She even spent a year in Brasília, the capital of Brazil, in a Christian drugs home. But she didn't have much intention of renouncing drugs; rather, her sole aim was to find shelter from Roberto, Grandão's brother. She owed him money, and would be finished off for it. The police wanted her dead rather than alive, and her own gang didn't trust her. So she thought it would be best if she disappeared for a while.

Cristina, a very helpful woman from Cesar's church, put her in touch with a rehabilitation centre in Brasília, and she went there. She organised hashish for herself from a nearby hut, had flings with a lot of the girls in the home, and when she found out after a few months that those who claimed to have turned Christian were let out earlier, she tried the same trick. She became a conscientious reader of the Bible and started preaching to the other girls how they should lead their lives. Her Christian disguise was so perfect that even Cesar's church believed in her conversion when, after a year, she returned to Ribeirão Preto with long hair and a long skirt, full of pious talk. Shannon was surprised by how easily she could convince these people of an inner change. When she spoke, she was even more pious than the pope himself, yet her heart was as hard as stone. But no one knew that. Only her.

The swindle only came to light a little later, when Shannon was attacked by a former buddy of hers. Under the circumstances, she finally admitted to Cristina that she was still involved in the drug trade and couldn't overcome her own addiction. The whole church was shocked. Once more, Cristina and Cesar offered her their help. Cristina took her in as if she were her own daughter, and Cesar met her regularly to talk with her. Unsuccessfully. After two months she was right back in hot water again. She wanted to get out. She really wanted to. But she didn't have the strength. The addiction was stronger than her will. It was as if the devil had her on a lead, and when she threatened to stray too far from him, he just tweaked on the lead and pulled her right back. There was no escape.

Four times over these five years Shannon had tried to take her own life. But even that didn't work. After one of her unsuccessful attempts she met up with Cesar, who commented strikingly: 'Living, dying, killing. For you it's all one and the same. It's time you finally woke up and started to live, Shannon. You can't keep on living like a corpse! God has a plan for you. Why don't you entrust him with your life? Why not?'

She didn't know why not. She just couldn't. Her life was too messed up. She had become immune to everything that came near her, immune to her own evil and even to God.

The next foolish mistake she made was the relationship with Josiane. Josiane had asked Shannon to give her English lessons, but after the second lesson it was clear where things were heading, and they let it happen. That Josiane suddenly wanted to end everything after three months and pour her heart out remorsefully to Cesar because her guilty conscience had caught up with her – well, that didn't suit Shannon one bit. After all, Josiane had known what she was getting into, and now she was going to have to bear the consequences.

'Know what I don't like about you Christians?' said Shannon, moving away from the window and pointing her index finger at Josiane. 'You're all a crowd of actors. You speak about God and hold moral sermons about what he thinks is all right and what not. But you don't actually follow those rules in real life. Shall I tell you something? When it comes down to it, your Christianity falls apart like a house of cards. The whole thing doesn't live up to its promise. It's all just empty words. Hypocrisy. Show me *one* Christian who's genuine, just one.'

'But, Shannon, even Christians make mistakes,' Josiane said in defence. 'I've made a mistake, getting involved with you. And now I'd like to settle it with God.'

'It's all so easy for you,' muttered Shannon. 'And what about me? If Cesar finds out about it …' She took a deep breath, and passed her right hand over her face. 'The cup's full, do you understand? I've let him down too many times already. Everyone has their limits. It's over. I can't live up to his expectations. He speaks about God's love, and I don't understand what he means. We're just too different from one another. We've been going down the same track for the past five years, and yet our rails don't ever cross. I tried to explain that to him in our last talk, four weeks ago. He just doesn't get it. And now if you go and tell him about our relationship, he'll write me off altogether.'

'I don't think he'll do that,' said Josiane, quite sure of herself.

Shannon shook her head. 'There's no point pretending to all of you and myself that I'll get there some day. Because I won't. I can't change who I am, and your God can't do that either.'

She turned around and left the room. She felt lousy. Why did everything she turned her hand to always fall apart? Why couldn't she do something good, just once? Cesar would be shocked. It's hard to have to admit that you spent five years investing in the wrong person. He'd probably given up on her long ago anyway, at the very latest since her last talk with him a month ago. Since then she hadn't gone to any services, and had made herself scarce at Cristina's as well.

Shannon spent the following two nights out on the street, by herself, huddled in a blanket she had found somewhere. She felt as though she was all alone in the world. Rejected. The dregs of society – for her family, the police, the drug dealers and her own gang, as well as for the church – and for Cesar. She was a nothing, and had herself to thank for it. She had played herself out. She had made a right botch-up of everything. Her whole life was one single scrap heap. And she couldn't expect anything more, neither from herself nor from anyone else.

The following day she went to Cristina, just to find out the lie of the land. When Shannon walked into Cristina's small apartment, the woman promptly spilled the coffee she was pouring.

'Shannon?! Where were you?' Cristina put the coffee pot back on the stove, wiped her hands on her apron and looked at the girl, shaking her head. 'It doesn't ever occur to you that we might be worried about you, does it? No, you prefer to disappear when things get sticky, isn't that right?'

'So you know, then,' muttered Shannon, not daring to look into Cristina's eyes.

Usually Cristina was a very good-tempered woman whom it was hard to ruffle. But for some reason she was pretty worked up, and her voice sounded anything other than gentle as she commented: 'Who do you actually think you are, Shannon?

People aren't simply objects you can take and throw away at your whim! Did you know that Cesar's mother has tuberculosis?' Shannon looked up in surprise. No, she hadn't known that.

'Yes, Shannon. Cesar's mother has tuberculosis, and he didn't even react when the doctors told him!'

'Why not?' asked Shannon, amazed.

'Why not?' repeated Cristina. 'Because he was so worried about *you*, Shannon! That's why!' She sighed, and passed the back of her hand over her forehead. 'Sorry I just came out with it like that. I just had to tell you, Shannon. Would you like a coffee?'

Shannon didn't reply. She was staring at Cristina open-mouthed, unable to utter a single word. The news had hit her like a bolt of lightning. Right in the middle of her heart. Cesar's mother had tuberculosis, and he wasn't worried about his mother – he was worried about a girl from the streets! A girl who lived on the streets and who had been nothing but a headache to him five years long! It was incredible. That there could be someone to whom she really meant so much was a feeling she had never experienced before. And even if there was only one Christian in the world who managed to incorporate God's love so perfectly, she had obviously found him here. This was no acting. This was genuine. And it made a greater impression on her than a thousand words. It was as if their rails had just crossed. She had to go and see him, right now. She had to speak to him.

'Shannon? I said would you like a coffee?'

'I have to go and see Cesar,' she said quietly, and with that she left Cristina's flat before she'd even properly entered it.

Cesar only lived a few streets down from her. Shannon made the journey in record time. Her heart was beating wildly as she stood at his door and knocked. Cesar opened the door, his eyelids drooping. He looked tired and pretty caught up with things. The rings under his eyes betrayed his lack of sleep over the last few nights. He was wearing washed-out jeans, a grey woollen pullover and slippers. When he saw Shannon at the door, his pale face lit up.

'Shannon?!' he cried happily. 'I was just praying for you.'

'You were praying for me?'

'I pray for you every day.'

'Every day?' said Shannon, overcome.

'Yes,' confirmed Cesar, 'because I know God still has a lot in store for you.' He patted her on the shoulder, and stood to one side. 'Come in. I'll make us a coffee.'

He led Shannon into his room. A Bible was lying on the table. Next to it were a pile of books, some papers and a prehistoric typewriter. Cesar shifted a pile of exercise books from one chair to another and told Shannon to take a seat, sitting down himself at the other side of the table.

'What made you come here?'

'I heard your mother is sick.'

'Tuberculosis,' said Cesar.

'I'm very sorry,' murmured Shannon.

'Is that why you came?'

'No, I . . . I've been thinking. I'd like . . .' She looked at Cesar. 'I'd like Jesus to change my life. I mean *really* change it.'

Cesar's hazel eyes began to shine. 'Shannon, that's the best decision of your life. You don't know how much I've been longing for this moment – and along with me, the whole of heaven.'

Shannon swallowed. She was beginning to feel warm inside. 'How … I mean, how do I go about it? I don't even know how to pray.'

The pastor smiled. 'Oh yes you do, Shannon. Praying means talking to God. Just tell him how you're feeling, tell him you are sorry for what you have done, and that you wish for nothing more than to let him into your heart.'

Shannon bit her lips, unsure. 'And what if he doesn't accept me? I mean, I'm far too bad for him. I've done everything wrong in my life. How can God possibly love someone like me?'

Cesar grabbed Shannon's hands and looked at her long and hard. 'Shannon. That's exactly why Jesus died on the cross. So that he could repair the destroyed bridge between God and his people. God loved the world so much that he gave it his only Son. He spilled his blood for every one of your sins. He has long since paid for them. He bought you your way out of death. And he loves you, Shannon. He loved you even before you were born. And he wants to heal your heart of all the wounds you have suffered, and he wants to free you from all the guilt you have built up over the years. Because he carried that guilt for you on the cross.'

Shannon nodded. She held Cesar's hands, and closed her eyes.

'Jesus,' she said in a quavering voice, and the lump in her throat grew bigger and bigger. 'Jesus, I can't take it much longer. I don't want to keep on living as I have done. Change me, Jesus! Take my ruined life and make it new again, if that's in any way possible, I give it to you. I give you everything that's left of me. Change me, Jesus, change me!'

A tear fell from her eyes and dropped on to the table. It was the first tear in eleven years. Shannon began to cry, for the first time since she was ten years old. And with each tear, a piece of dirt fell from her soul. The spell had been broken. The curse had been lifted. Something strange was happening inside her. The terrible weight that she had been carrying around with her for so many years, getting heavier and heavier, fell away, as if she were stepping out of iron armour. She cried like a little child, she gulped out the hatred, the suffering, all the atrocities she had committed over the past eleven years, and laid them at Jesus' feet. And with each admission of guilt to God, with each word she screamed out in desperation to Jesus, her heart felt a little less burdened, and a deep joy and indescribable warmth streamed through her like a godly fire. It was the most powerful experience she had ever had. Jesus was slowly healing her. And when she looked into Cesar's light brown eyes, she knew that the light in his eyes was now also in hers. The same light that she had marvelled at in Nicolas' clear green eyes was at that moment shining out of hers. God had worked a miracle.

19

Carrying the torch of love

Shannon had never felt so light and unburdened. No drug in the world could replace how she felt. She was filled with boundless relief and deep joy. The glowing ember, which the devil had tried for the last twenty-one years to blow out, had caught fire. And it was a fire that hopefully would never again die, because God himself had kindled it. Shannon felt the flame burning inside her, right in the very centre of her heart, and her tears were mixed with laughter. She could have hugged the whole world. But because only Cesar was present, and not the whole world, she hugged him, almost winding the kindly pastor with her fierce embrace.

'Hey, Shannon, are you trying to kill me?!' he gasped, and when she let go, he wiped his eyes with his sleeve.

'Thank you,' was all Shannon could say, beaming at the pastor. 'Thank you, Cesar.'

'Thank God!' he replied, passing on the laurel wreath and raising his eyes to heaven. 'I'm just one of the fallible ground staff.'

'You prayed for me.'

'Ah well,' said Cesar dismissively. 'The strength for it came from God. Right from the beginning, he somehow made it clear to me that I had to take you on and then hang on in there. I just felt that God still has great plans for you, Shannon. I just know it. Don't ask me why. But I knew it right from the moment I saw you for the first time, five years ago.' He placed his hand on her shoulder. 'You're something special, Shannon. Your story will convert lots of people, believe me.'

'I hope so,' nodded Shannon, and as she did so she felt that God's love was streaming through her, through her whole body, from the top of her head down into her smallest toe. God loved her – her, and the whole human race. It was crazy! Shannon couldn't get over it. And she was prepared to carry the torch of love further, out into the darkness of the world, which she herself knew so well.

She would give it her all. She would not keep quiet about what God had done in her heart. She would tell everyone who was prepared to listen: Jesus Christ had invaded her heart! It was so incredible that she herself could barely grasp it. It had just happened. And if God could clearly get on so well with a murderer and a criminal of the very worst sort, then he could cope with everyone, really everyone.

In spite of the incredible turnaround in her life, Shannon naturally still had to keep on fighting the problems that God hadn't simply swept away. One of her greatest difficulties was getting over the drugs. Ridding herself of the addiction was a long, exhausting process. Her body had been addicted to the poison for many years and was now practically screaming out for it; giving it up was hard, very hard, and took many months. When she had one of her fits, was plagued with bouts of shivering, cramps, muscular pain and depression, and became so aggressive that she would cheerfully have destroyed everything around her, then she tried to concentrate on God and prayed until the fit was over. Cesar, Cristina and many others stood faithfully by her throughout this torturous time of healing.

Another serious problem to be solved was Shannon's ties to demonic forces. Ever since she had first made her pact with the devil at the age of eleven, she had carried out an attack on the first day of every month and delivered up a sacrifice to Satan. Giving up this habit alone was anything other than easy. There were nights when Shannon was strangled or beaten by invisible hands, so that on the following morning she could barely stand up straight. She could feel the presence of the dark powers; sometimes she saw them in the flesh, and sometimes the spirits even possessed her body. For three days and three nights a good few Christians prayed intensively in a church for Shannon's release from these ties.

Once a week Shannon met up with Cesar, and he helped her to understand the Bible better, along with God's wish for her life, and then showed her how to act in accordance with this. There were a lot of hurdles to overcome. Sometimes Shannon felt like a little child, holding on to its father's hand and braving the first hesitant steps. On other occasions, driven by God's overpowering love, she felt completely capable of conjuring up the devil and standing firm against him.

There were also moments when Shannon was struck down and plagued by terrible feelings of guilt. The thought of having the lives of so many people weighing on her conscience almost made her crazy for a while. She was prepared to stand up and face the consequences for it, yes. But no prison sentence in the world would bring back all the people that she had killed so early on in her life. A lawyer checked out the legal situation, and decided there wasn't any point in Shannon handing herself over to the police, especially as Shannon could barely remember the details of the individual crimes and most of them had been committed years ago. On top of that, she'd already spent so long in prison, and suffered under the most terrible methods of torture, that she had probably done more than her time for the deeds. And if a prison sentence was supposed to re-socialise the prisoner, then this aim had already been achieved by Shannon's radical turnaround.

And yet, despite the lawyer's reassuring words, the feelings of guilt continued to burn in Shannon's heart, and sometimes she thought she was going to choke on them. Often, when Cesar mentioned the existence of hell in one of his sermons, she was suddenly seized by a terrible panic, and began to doubt that Jesus had really forgiven her for all of her shocking crimes. It just wasn't possible that he could have forgiven her *everything*, not when she had carried out such horrific, bloody deeds – deeds that filled even her with naked horror when she thought back to them. And Jesus was supposed to have forgiven her for all that? Without receiving anything in return from her? Was he really that merciful?

One day, when she was turning around these thoughts in her heart after a service, she suddenly thought she could hear an inner voice telling her: 'Shannon, you can't blame yourself for something I've already paid for. What you did was bad. But I paid for it with my death. If you keep on accusing yourself, you will take from the greatness of my deed on the cross. It is over, Shannon. Once and for all. I died for all of humankind's sins. It is over.'

Shannon began to cry when she realised the truth of these words. It was as if God had cleansed her heart for a second time. Finally. 'It is over!' Jesus had cried out on the cross, before he died. And it was as if Jesus was uttering this victory cry once more, right in the middle of Shannon's life, and she now no longer doubted the truth of these words: 'It is over.'

★ ★ ★

A few weeks after her conversion, Shannon met a beggar on the street. He was probably about forty, had red, watery eyes, greasy hair and an unkempt beard. He was sitting on a wall in front of a house, wearing dirty, ragged clothes and surrounded by an almost unbearable stink of urine. He stretched his dirt-encrusted hand out to Shannon.

'A réal,' he begged the girl, 'just one réal.'

Shannon stopped in front of him. 'I've got something better,' she said spontaneously. 'Do you know Jesus?'

The man took back his hand. His face darkened. 'Just don't start up with that,' he growled. 'What do you know about life out on the street?'

'I know all about it,' Shannon explained. 'I spent eleven years on the street. Do you know the park in the town centre? That used to be my home. But you know what? Since I realised that Jesus loves me, my life has changed completely. And the best thing is: Jesus loves you, too.'

'You don't know what you're talking about,' retorted the beggar irately. 'Jesus loves me? Like hell he does! See my leg here? I'd like to know if you're brave enough to have a look at it. Have a look, if you think you can! And then we can talk about this so-called love!'

He pointed to his right leg. He had stretched it out: both foot and shin were wrapped in a dirty bandage.

'Seven shots,' he said, and his eyes flashed with anger. 'I jumped over a wall, and the pigs shot at me. Seven shots. They punctured my foot like a sieve. So come on, then, have a look at it before you start preaching about love.'

Shannon hesitated.

The man looked at her challengingly, waiting eagerly for her reaction. 'Afraid, aren't you?'

Shannon knew he was trying to test her. She knelt down

next to him decisively, and wordlessly began to unwind the filthy, blood-smeared bandage from his leg. She forced herself not to look away in disgust. The sight of the foot, shot to pieces, was horrific; the foul stench nearly made her throw up. Shannon was used to a lot. Once a corpse had lain in their hideout for several days before they had thrown him into the river on a foggy night. But looking at this swollen, pus-filled foot needed a lot of self-control.

'That shuts you up, doesn't it?' cackled the beggar in satisfaction. 'And you come along and want to tell me about love? Don't make me laugh!'

'Know what I think?' said Shannon, looking into the man's watery eyes. 'This wound may be disgusting. But it's nothing compared to the wound that you've got in your heart and that Jesus would like to heal.'

The beggar's jaw hit the floor. This remark had hit home. Right on the bull's-eye. She had put her finger right on the sore spot.

'Jesus loves you,' Shannon repeated. 'He gave his life for you. He let himself be flogged for the love of you. He let nails be drilled through him for the love of you. He let himself be hammered to the cross for the whole world's sins. That's how much he loves us. He gave me a new life, and he can do the same for you. He can heal that oozing wound in your heart.'

The beggar grabbed Shannon's arm. And suddenly his eyes filled with tears, and this man, a minute ago so bitter, now began to cry. 'I feel so lousy,' he whispered through his tears. 'Pray for me. Please, pray for me.'

Shannon did, and the beggar kept a strong hold on her arm throughout, crying all the time. It was a solemn moment, and when Shannon had finished her prayer the man said a loud and heartfelt 'Amen'. A deep satisfaction shone in his face.

'I think,' said Shannon, looking critically at the injured leg,

237

'you'd be better off showing that to a doctor. If you agree, I'll call an ambulance.'

The beggar nodded thankfully. 'You're a godsend,' he murmured, and didn't want to let go of the girl. 'You must be an angel, or something.'

Shannon waved it off, smiling. 'I'm nothing. Jesus is everything. Hold on to him, him alone. Don't ever lose sight of him, never.' She freed her arm from his hand and got up. 'I'm going to call an ambulance now, okay?'

The ambulance came shortly. At first the ambulance men refused to even touch the lumpy, stinking down-and-out, but Shannon spoke so long to their conscience that they overcame their disgust and lifted the beggar into the vehicle. The man didn't want to be parted from Shannon, but she promised to visit him in hospital as soon as possible.

'You're a godsend,' he said over and over again. 'God bless you, my child.'

Shannon nodded to him, then the ambulance men closed the back doors and drove off. Shannon watched thoughtfully as the white vehicle disappeared into the distance, and then looked at the empty piece of cardboard the beggar had been sitting on only minutes ago. For a moment, she thought maybe she had just dreamed the whole incident.

It was unbelievable. She had helped someone. She, she who had only recently shot at people without hesitating, and who had watched people die at her own hand and not felt anything as they passed away, she was now telling an injured beggar about Jesus! And the most amazing thing was, he had listened to her! And he had even asked her to pray for him! Wasn't that pretty crazy? It wasn't just crazy, it was sensational!

Shannon could barely believe that all this had just happened. God had used her. He had put the right words into her mouth. He had made her a torch-bearer for his love – her, of all people.

It filled her with great joy, and also a certain amount of self-belief and healthy pride. Obviously she had a gift with down-and-outs and knew how to talk to them. Perhaps that was her strength. She decided to talk to Cesar about it.

That Sunday, after the service, she took him to one side and told him excitedly about the encounter with the beggar and her idea of somehow trying to help those on the edge of society. Cesar thought it an excellent idea.

'I've got a fine task for you there,' he said, placing his arm paternally around her shoulder. 'How about providing company for AIDS victims in hospital?'

'*What* did you just say?' Shannon thought she hadn't heard right. 'Are you crazy?'

'Hey, I'm serious,' repeated Cesar. 'You know what we do with AIDS victims. We care for them in our home as long as it's in any way possible. As soon as we realise that they're on their way out, we take them to the hospital where a special team looks after them until their death. You'd be the ideal person to help the dying. It's not macabre or anything. I think God could really use you there.'

'And what gives you that idea?'

'How many times have you looked death in the eye, Shannon? How often have you fought with those thoughts that occupy a person facing death? You know what goes on there, you know it from personal experience. And that's why they'll listen to you, just like the beggar listened to you.'

Shannon shook her head. 'I don't know, Cesar. I think that one's beyond me.'

The pastor didn't give up so easily. 'Do you know what the really great thing about our God is? He's always got more in store for us than we would ordinarily have of our own accord. He genuinely believes us capable of more than we ourselves do. Sometimes he even expects more of us than we would take on of our own volition. That's what makes life as a Christian so exciting.'

Shannon shrugged her shoulders. 'All the same. What am I supposed to say to them?'

Cesar opened his big black Bible, leafed through it and read out verses 19 and 20 of the tenth chapter of Matthew's Gospel: 'But when they arrest you, do not worry about what to say or how to say it. At that time you will be given what to say, for it will not be you speaking, but the Spirit of your Father speaking through you.' He clapped the Bible shut and gave Shannon a wink of encouragement. 'You'll find the right words, Shannon, no doubt about it. So what about it: are you going to take it on?'

She bit her lip, and considered. Essentially, she knew that Cesar was quite right. If anyone knew about the inner battles of someone facing death, then she did. Should she risk it? It was an enormous challenge. She probably couldn't find a harder task. And yet what she most wanted was to help people who were in similar situations to those in which she had once been. So why shouldn't she try and comfort patients dying of AIDS? Didn't these people need Jesus just as much as others? Or perhaps even more?

'Okay,' she decided bravely, 'I'll try it.'

It soon became clear that Shannon was received incredibly well by the AIDS victims, most of whom were still young, and she achieved far more than she had ever expected. The patients poured their hearts out to Shannon and spoke of their fear of death. And Shannon took their fear from them. Many a decision was made on the final night. People accepted Jesus Christ as their lord just before they breathed their last. Many tears were shed, tears of joy, tears of release, tears of wonder at the immeasurable greatness and goodness of Jesus. Amazing things happened. Shannon became the messenger of God's love in the face of death. She scattered seeds of hope in the midst of despair, joy in the midst of sorrow, peace in the midst of fear, freedom in the midst of the world of the bedridden, those who were confined to a space just the size of a mattress.

Once she converted not only a girl terminally ill with AIDS but also her parents, whom Shannon visited on several occasions. And at the funeral, the parents introduced Shannon to all their friends and relatives, and said, their eyes brimming with tears: 'This is the girl who was at our daughter's side throughout her last night.'

Two months later, on one of her hospital visits Shannon chanced across Cat, her former best friend in the underworld. The boy with Japanese facial features and different-coloured eyes was little more than a skeleton, and you didn't have to be a doctor to tell he wouldn't live much longer. He was a pitiful sight, especially for Shannon, who knew how much energy he had once possessed. None of that was left now. The deadly illness had eaten him up. Shannon began to visit him regularly, and read to him from the Bible. He was impressed by the obvious change in her life, but didn't want to have anything to do with it himself.

But one day, after the person in the bed next to him had died, everything suddenly looked quite different. The panic in Cat's face was obvious as he grabbed hold of Shannon's arm and whispered in a quivering voice: 'I'm next.' His nostrils flared in dismay, his eyes were desperately seeking some kind of support in hers. 'I'm afraid, Shannon,' he admitted, his face pale as a ghost. 'I'm not yet ready to die. Do you understand? I have nightmares. I see the demons of the night, hunched over there in the corner and grinning, waiting to come and get me. I don't want to go to hell! I'm so terribly frightened, Shannon! So terribly frightened!'

Shannon remembered the time when together they had made the streets of Ribeirão Preto unsafe. She remembered a businessman who had owed them money and who had fallen shaking to his knees, begging them for mercy. They had murdered him in cold blood. Mercy was something for weaklings, not for the hardened likes of Shannon or Cat.

Who would ever have thought, then, that one day all that would change? Who would ever have thought that one day even the stony, heartless Cat would plead for mercy in the face of death? Not even Cat, once feared by everybody, could hide away his real fears now that he was about to pass through the gates of eternity. The cool, self-assured mask fell away, and his bony face was filled with the fear of hell.

'Help me, Shannon!' he pleaded, not letting go of her. 'Help me!'

Shannon knew there was no religion, no philosophy, no human wisdom that could help her former friend. There is only one person who can offer a real hope to people even when they are dying: Jesus Christ. Shannon pulled out her Bible and opened it at Luke chapter 23.

'Two other men, both criminals, were also led out with him to be executed. When they came to the place called the Skull, there they crucified him, along with the criminals – one on his right, the other on his left. One of the criminals who hung there hurled insults at him: "Aren't you the Christ? Save yourself and us!" But the other criminal rebuked him. "Don't you fear God," he said, "since you are under the same sentence? We are punished justly, for we are getting what our deeds deserve. But this man has done nothing wrong." Then he said, "Jesus, remember me when you come into your kingdom." Jesus answered him, "I tell you the truth, today you will be with me in paradise." '

Shannon clapped the Bible shut, and looked smilingly at Cat.

'Do you understand, Cat?' she asked him. 'It's still not too late to change your mind. Jesus himself promised the criminal on the cross shortly before his death that he would go with him to Paradise. The guy was probably just as despicable a rat as you were in your life. Probably a brutal serial killer. And yet Jesus forgave him, purely and simply because this murderer believed that Jesus was the Son of God.' She gave Cat a friendly punch in the side. 'The same goes for you, mate! Do you understand? You don't need to fear death. Give your life over to Jesus, admit your guilt to him, let him cleanse your life. There's still time!'

Cat listened attentively to Shannon. He didn't ask any questions. He just listened, and when Shannon asked him whether he would like to give his life over to Jesus Christ, he answered, 'Yes.' A look of peace settled on his face after he had prayed with Shannon. It was as if his fear had been blown away. It was an unforgettable moment.

From now on, Shannon visited her friend every day to read the Bible with him. On the night he died, Shannon was watching over his bed, and saw once again how the encounter with the living God of the Bible gave even a person in his last hours courage and confidence, something which was far beyond all logical comprehension and knowledge. Cat had found his way home. And Shannon was happy that she had been able to show an old friend the way into life.

Shannon had incredible experiences providing company for the patients dying of AIDS. One day she was called over to a girl called Patricia who was tied to the bed because she had tried to kill herself. A girl was lying next to her whose head was swollen like a balloon as a result of a tumour. Shannon shuddered somewhat at the sight of this girl. She looked like some sort of extra-terrestrial from a sci-fi movie, with her small eyes and over-large head. Nevertheless, Shannon managed to get the better of herself and smiled at the girl in greeting.

'Hello, I'm Shannon. I'm going to spend the night here.'

'I'm Priscilla,' said the girl quietly, not moving. After Shannon had talked for a while with Patricia, she sat and began to read the Bible until a nurse turned out the light. Then Shannon curled up on the floor next to Patricia's bed, as she had already done hundreds of times before in this room for victims dying of AIDS, and soon fell asleep.

In the middle of the night, she was shocked out of her sleep. She could hear someone groaning. It was Priscilla. She was clearly in pain. Shannon got up and went over to her. Silvery moonlight was coming through the closed window, making Priscilla's head look even more ghostly than it was anyway. Shannon pulled herself together and didn't let it bother her. After all, the girl couldn't help the way she looked.

'Shall I call the nurse for you?' asked Shannon.

'It's all right,' said Priscilla. 'It's almost passed.'

Shannon took her hand and held on to it.

The girl looked over at her thankfully through her tiny eyes. 'Are you a Christian?'

Shannon nodded.

'I saw you reading the Bible,' said Priscilla. 'I … I used to be a Christian too.'

'Used to be?' repeated Shannon questioningly. 'Does that mean you're not any more?'

'Just look at me,' mumbled the girl in shame. 'Do I look like a Christian?'

'What's that got to do with it?'

'I turned my back on God.' Priscilla explained without emotion. 'I sinned. And God punished me for it with AIDS. There's no hope for me any more.'

Shannon could sense the despair in the young girl's words.

'Hey,' she said, taking a tighter hold of Priscilla's hand. 'God's world is a world of hope. If God had punished me for everything I've done, I wouldn't be here today, believe you me. But I am. God gave me a second chance. And he's always giving me fresh chances, every day. Because every day I always do something that makes me guilty, something that I say or something that I think. None of us is perfect, not even the most pious Christian. But do you know what John says about this to the Christians in his first letter? Wait a moment, I'll read it to you.' She fetched her Bible, opened it at the right place and read by the light of the moon: 'My dear children, I write this to you so that you will not sin. But if anybody does sin, we have one who speaks to the Father in our defence – Jesus Christ, the Righteous One. He is the atoning sacrifice for our sins, and not only for ours but also for the sins of the whole world.' Shannon looked at Priscilla. 'Do you believe that?'

The girl felt for her hand. 'Would you ... could you pray for me, Shannon?'

Shannon nodded. 'Of course.' She placed the Bible on the white blanket, took hold of Priscilla's cold, bony hands, and closed her eyes. 'Jesus. I ask you: give Priscilla renewed hope. Show her how much you love her. Let her feel that you are with her and have long since forgiven her. She needs you so much, Jesus. Give her a sign of your love, so that she knows she is safe with you in all her suffering, in all her pain, in all the guilt that you have long since buried in the depths of the deepest ocean and which you yourself have long since paid for. Take Priscilla in your strong, loving hands. This I ask of you, Father. Amen.'

When she opened her eyes again, she saw tears in Priscilla's eyes. She stroked her cheek softly. 'I don't know if God will heal your body, Priscilla. But one thing you must know: even if he doesn't heal you on the outside, your soul is nevertheless safe with him. Don't ever forget that.'

'Thank you,' breathed Priscilla, fixing Shannon with her small, shining eyes, and not moving. 'You don't know what a help you've been to me.'

When Shannon came to visit Priscilla a week later, she was no longer there. But a nurse reported that two days before her death a wonder had happened: the swelling on her head had mysteriously disappeared, and Priscilla had wanted to thank Shannon for this, and to let her know that now she knew her soul was safe.

Shannon couldn't find any words to describe what she felt in her heart when the nurse passed on this message to her. She was simply blown away by the way God had responded to her prayer. He had given Priscilla a sign of his love. A prickling kind of joy overcame Shannon, a reverent amazement at God's mercy. How boundlessly merciful was this God, whose child she could call herself. How boundlessly good. How eternally great. How near to all who called to him, all who seriously called to him.

20

And again: Father!

Shannon's conversion had a radical effect on her life, and the love of God that filled her heart to bursting point spread out in ever wider circles. Shannon took up a job as an English teacher, and moved by her story, Luiz Fernando, a colleague from work, also decided to commit his life to Jesus. Earlier, he and Shannon had taken drugs together; now they met every morning, afternoon and evening to pray together for the school. When ten further teachers, struck by their example, also became Christians, the school principal felt so uncomfortable that he fired Shannon. She didn't let it bother her, and soon found another job in a different school of English.

In her spare time, she carried on visiting the AIDS victims and told her story in various churches and schools. Wherever she went, God used her life to change people's hearts.

She learned to play the guitar and began writing songs. Guitar in one hand, Bible in the other, she set off to carry God's love into the young offenders' prisons. Working with criminals meant a lot to her. She saw herself in those teenage faces filled with hatred and violence. She knew how these young people thought, and she knew who could fill the emptiness in their lives.

In one of the prisons, initially only four inmates took part in the events Shannon organised alone, but the number of interested people soon rose to over fifty. On one afternoon nineteen young people gave their lives over to Jesus – and Shannon had done nothing more than sing a few of her songs on the guitar and tell her story. But God was there. And he was working. In the middle of the prison. No place was too dingy for him. He didn't let anything get in the way of saving people.

Shannon had no qualms about telling someone about Jesus and the effect he had had on her life. There was only one person Shannon couldn't meet with the enthusiastic love Jesus had given her.

Her father.

The wounds her father had inflicted on her throughout her life were too deep to heal just like that. When Shannon met him for the first time in over seven years in her grandparents' house, he acted as if she didn't exist, and she could only feel the deepest contempt for everything he had done to her. Many people prophesied that grass would grow over it all in time, but these prophecies were not fulfilled. Quite the opposite. Shannon's hatred for her father grew stronger whenever she thought of him. Sometimes it made her so aggressive that she would have liked to attack total strangers out on the street.

During a church event where Shannon was supposed to tell stories from her life, she learned that her father was visiting her grandparents. The news hit her like a bolt of lightning. Her hands involuntarily clenched themselves into fists. Her pulse hit 180. A terrible thought shot through her head – a thought she didn't dare think through to the end. But she had made up her mind to do 'it'.

The service had only just begun, with a few modern, rhythmical songs. The people were crowded into the over-full church and were praising God with applause and dancing. Shannon couldn't take the music any longer. Everything seemed to be spinning in front of her. She thought she could hear a hoarse voice whispering in her ear: 'Do what you have to do quickly!' Her heart was beating wildly. She ran from the church, quaking with hatred and confusion at her own terrible thoughts. She took a deep breath of fresh air, and tried to get hold of herself again.

Suddenly she felt a hand on her shoulder. Turning around, she saw Cesar standing across from her, shaking his head and looking at her lovingly.

'Shannon. I know what you're planning. Don't do it.'

Shannon pushed his hand from her shoulder. 'Leave me alone!' she growled. 'It's none of your business.'

'You're playing with the idea of killing your father, aren't you?'

Shannon stared at him.

'God showed me your intentions,' the pastor explained simply. 'Don't do it, Shannon. Don't go to him. Not with this intention in your heart.'

'I said it's none of your business!' growled Shannon.

'Shannon,' said Cesar, and his voice was soft and understanding, 'you know that's not the solution. You have to forgive your father, just as Jesus forgave you. *That* is the strength of God. Forgiveness.'

'That's all very easy for you to say,' countered Shannon. 'You don't know what he did to me.'

'Jesus was nailed to the cross, and said: "Father, forgive them, for they know not what they do." '

'I'm not Jesus!'

'But you are his follower. And his message is: "Love your enemies. Bless those who curse you. Do good to those who hate you." All the time you don't forgive your father, you won't find peace.'

'I can't forgive him,' groaned Shannon. 'First *he* has to ask me for forgiveness. And he'll never do that. I know my dad.'

'Then ask God to work a miracle,' Cesar suggested. 'Ask him to tear the hatred from your heart *and* change your dad. For God, nothing is impossible – and you should know that even better than me.' He gave her a friendly slap on the shoulder. 'At least give it a go, okay?'

Shannon took a deep breath, and nodded, pretty unconvinced. 'Okay.'

A few days later, Shannon rang her grandparents and told them she would like to come and see her father. She wanted to talk to him.

The following afternoon – on 6th February 1995 – she approached the house where her father was staying with mixed feelings. She hadn't the faintest idea how she should meet him. She was afraid she would suddenly lose her nerve, that the encounter would end in disaster. When she saw red, no one was able to stop her. She knew what she was like, and she knew her explosive temperament. She had to fight it enough as it was. One stupid remark from her father and she would lose it. She was frightened of her own temper. She was frightened of being disappointed by her father yet again, and these conflicting feelings churned in her stomach like a fist turning around and around inside her. Her feet were heavy as lead as she approached the house. A lump was tightening in her throat.

'Oh, God,' she prayed inwardly, 'I can't go through with this. Do something, or I'm going to flip! You know me. I can't love my dad, I can't do it, not even if I wanted to!'

She put her foot on the doorstep. And then something incredible, something overpowering happened, something for which Shannon couldn't find any words: she saw a bright light. And a hand tore something out of her heart. The whole thing didn't even last three seconds, and no sooner had it happened than Shannon wondered whether maybe she'd just imagined it all. But when she entered her grandparents' house, she suddenly realised that something inside her had changed. No, she wasn't imagining it or inventing it. It was a fact: her hatred was gone! Simply gone. Not there any more. Vanished into thin air. Just like that.

Before she could begin to wonder about what had actually happened, she had already entered the sitting room.

And he was standing there.

Her father.

He was standing at the window and had his back turned to her.

'Dad?' murmured Shannon timidly, standing stock-still. He turned around. For a short moment, Shannon saw herself taken back fourteen years to the time when she had landed with Aunt Carolina at the airport in Minneapolis, where her father, wearing his long, dark blue winter coat, had collected her. That was fourteen years ago. And in all that time, her father had barely changed at all: tall, strong, short-cropped hair, dark eyes, washed-out jeans and trainers. She remembered how she had met him with such expectation back then, a thin nine-year-old girl who had longed for nothing more than to be hugged by her father. Even today she could feel the tingling feeling in her stomach, the childishly naive expectation that her father would be a real dad, a dad like the ones in the picture books, a loving, perfect dad, a dad who took time to care for his child's needs and who was always ready with advice and help.

Fourteen years had passed. Fourteen years in which *none* of that had happened, none of what Shannon aged nine had hoped for from her dad. Nobody would have been able to simply erase all the bitter disappointments that had built up over those fourteen years. Nobody could take away what had happened. And yet: something had happened. Something for which there was no logical explanation. It was as if God had erased those entries written in blood and tears on the pages that represented the last fourteen years of Shannon's life.

Shannon looked at her father, and it was as if all her spite, all her hatred, all her painful memories had been rubbed out, just as if she and her father had never had an argument! Just like that, as if the page that documented their common story was still empty, completely white! Only God could do such a thing. And he had, as it turned out, done even more.

'Shannon,' mumbled her father, approaching his twenty-three-year-old daughter hesitantly. Their eyes met, and Shannon saw that something had changed in her father's eyes. They were no longer the same arrogant, self-righteous eyes that Shannon knew from earlier times; they were eyes that mirrored regret and shame, the watery eyes of a broken man who had realised his guilt and didn't know if he could ever make good what he had done wrong.

Shannon's heart beat wildly. Her father came up to her, at first slowly and timidly and then quickly and decisively, and when he hugged her tight in his arms the last remnants of ice between them melted away.

'I'm so sorry about everything that happened between us,' murmured her father. Tears were streaming down his face. He held Shannon in his arms as if he never wanted to let her go again. 'I'm so very, very sorry.'

'I'm sorry too, Dad,' Shannon managed, completely surprised by his reaction, as the tears ran down her cheeks as well. 'I'm really sorry, Dad.'

They didn't say anything more. Nothing more was necessary right then. They had found each other again.

After more than fourteen years.

God had given them another chance.

They stood there for a long time, in a tight embrace, wordless, overcome, and completely forgetting the time. Then they sat on the sofa and spent the whole afternoon talking to one another. They spoke of things that they had never spoken of before. They cleared up everything which needed to be cleared up. They laughed together, they cried together, they poured their hearts out to one another, far more openly and honestly than Shannon could ever have expected. She felt God's presence more strongly than ever. It was one of the most beautiful, liberating days in her whole life. She and her father were reconciled.

And the reconciliation written on their faces shone brighter than the evening sun coming in through the window.

Much brighter.

> Father,
> All of me
> Stands in your presence.
> There is no other God
> In this universe.
> You are
> The crystal clear spring of peace and love;
> When I look at you
> I shake with awe:
> *TETELESTAI*
> IT IS OVER!

There were moments of fear
When the street threatened to swallow me up;
But your mercy was my saviour.
Jesus,
Indescribable love,
On the cross you showed the impossible,
You paid for my sins with your flesh
And out of love for us all
You shouted out loudly:
TETELESTAI
IT IS OVER!

(*Translation of a song Shannon wrote after she realised the true greatness of Jesus' deed on the cross.*)

Afterword

Shannon – one of God's miracles.

For every fifty boys who manage to find their way back from the street into a normal life, there is only one girl. Fifty to one – a shocking ratio. The reason for this is that girls carry far greater inner hurt with them than street boys. Working with girls out on the street is incredibly difficult. I really have known very few girls who managed to make the break. But this is not about measuring success in figures. God doesn't make history with figures – rather with people. And the effect God has had on Shannon's life is unique. Shannon is living proof of the fact that for God there are no hopeless cases. I realise this every time I meet her.

In 1997 I lived in the same building in São Paulo as Shannon. Her exuberance made a deep impression on me. She took me with her out on to the street and into the young offenders' prison. The young people respond to her friendly manner. They know her and are always happy when she comes. Shannon is even partly 'responsible' for my own involvement with street children. It was Shannon who said to me in 1996: 'Come back, Damaris. We need people like you here.'

In the meantime, Shannon has started attending a Bible school near São Paulo. In her free time she carries on visiting prisons, writing songs and being active in the church. She wants to stretch out a hand to those who are in the same difficulties as she once was. I think Shannon is just the right person for this task, and I hope that her story will show many more people the way to Jesus.

Damaris Kofmehl

The story continues …

Damaris Kofmehl has been actively involved with street children since 1997. She continues to help out in the Salvation Army's night project *coração* in São Paulo, and has just become engaged in a dental project run by the Swiss charity CHildrenAID in São Paulo and Rio de Janeiro (more about these two projects below).

Anyone who would like to contact Damaris Kofmehl directly can do so at the following addresses:

Damaris Kofmehl
Rua José Ferreira da Rocha, 39
Liberdade
01508-040 São Paulo
Brazil
e-mail: kofmehl@hotmail.com

Contact address in Switzerland:
Berty Kofmehl
Niederweg 103
CH-8907 Wettswil
Switzerland
e-mail: kofmehl@bluewin.ch

The Salvation Army's night project *coracão*

The street children project *coracão* was founded by the captain of the Swiss Salvation Army in June 1996. A maximum of twenty boys aged between seven and seventeen who show the desire to get off the streets can find night-time accommodation here. The project gives them somewhere to shower, wash their clothes, play games, have dinner and sleep. And every evening they hear the word of God. In addition, they have the chance of getting into a home for twelve boys. Here they live as if in a family and can go to school again. Through this project many have already found their way back into society and a better life – and, not least, the way to God.

Donations to:

Switzerland
Die Heilsarmee (Salvation Army)
Postfach 6575
CH-3001 Bern
Postal account: 30-3117-4
FAO: Mission, *coracão* project, São Paulo

Germany
Heilsarmee Köln (Cologne Salvation Army)
Bank für Sozialwirtschaft
Sorting code: 370 205 00
Account number: 40 777 00
FAO: Mission, *coracão* project, São Paulo

Dental project CHildrenAID

Police officer Jürg Steiner and dentist Dr Jürg Widmer are involved in providing free dental treatment for Brazilian street children. As a group on the edge of society, these children normally have no access to professional dental care.

The aim of the charity CHildrenAID is to open modern dental clinics in both São Paulo and Rio de Janeiro.

Donations to:

CHildrenAID
Postfach 516
CH-8703 Erlenbach
Switzerland
PC-Account number: 87-171717-3

Other Christian testimonies published by
Hodder & Stoughton include:

A Cop for Christ

The Dramatic True Story of Mike DiSanza of the NYPD

'I looked around and saw the people of New York, my people, with their faces set in cold worried lines, their bodies bent against the problems life had thrown at them. I stepped forward and lifted the bullhorn to my mouth. This time my voice rang out, "Listen up, I've got some good news . . ."'

Officer Mike DiSanza of the New York Police Department was a cop just like any other, patrolling the subways and streets of Harlem, when a near-death experience led to an amazing turnaround in his perception of the world around him. He discovered a new message of hope and compassion for all of God's people and a new call on his own career.

A Cop for Christ tells Mike's dramatic story, from his growing up in the Bronx, New York, through more than twenty-two gritty years with the NYPD and his astonishing ministry taking the love of Jesus to people who know life only as a struggle for survival.

ISBN 0 340 78519 5

Our Little Secret

My Life in the Shadow of Abuse

Tori Dante
with Julia Fisher

This is the harrowing story of Tori Dante, wife of the World Wide Message Tribe's Cameron Dante, and of the regular sexual abuse inflicted on her by her father. It describes her journey from the despair of her childhood to the healing she discovered after committing her life to Jesus. It has been written, with the help of writer and broadcaster Julia Fisher, to inspire all readers and will be of particular help to anyone who has suffered abuse themselves, or to those who are close to them.

'This book is shocking . . . we dare not ignore it.'
Rob Parsons

'This graphic and moving account is a challenge to us all. Would your church have listened and obtained the help Tori needed, both as a child and an adult?'
CCPAS (Churches' Child Protection Advisory Service)

'I know her [Tori's] deeply disturbing story needs to be told and hope that many will find comfort through it.'
Andy Hawthorne, The Tribe

ISBN 0 340 78590 X

The Street Children of Brazil

One Woman's Remarkable Story

Sarah de Carvalho

Her glittering career in film promotion and
TV production took her to California, Sydney and
London. But her international lifestyle and fast-lane
salary gave her no time to enjoy herself.

Through a series of remarkable events, Sarah left her
career and joined a missionary organisation in
Brazil. There she met children from the age of
seven living on the streets, taking drugs, stealing
to survive and open to prostitution and
gang warfare.

This is the remarkable true story of a life transformed. It
tells of the incredible work that Sarah de Carvalho and
her husband have founded in the Happy
Child Mission. It is a story of immense faith,
suffering and love. The children whose stories are
revealed in this exceptional book will change
the heart of every reader.

ISBN 0 340 64164 9